Alcoholism Counseling

Alcoholism Counseling

ISSUES FOR AN EMERGING PROFESSION

By

STEPHEN K. VALLE, Sc.D.

Chief of Psychology
Mount Pleasant Hospital
Director of Psychological Services
American International Health Services
Lynn, Massachusetts

With a Foreword by

Harold E. Hughes

U.S. Senate, Retired

CHARLES C THOMAS • PUBLISHER
Springfield • Illinois • U.S.A.

Published and Distributed Throughout the World by

CHARLES C THOMAS ● PUBLISHER

Bannerstone House

301-327 East Lawrence Avenue, Springfield, Illinois, U.S.A.

© *1979, by* CHARLES C THOMAS ● PUBLISHER

ISBN 0-398-03877-5

Library of Congress Catalog Card Number: 78-23726

With THOMAS BOOKS *careful attention is given to all details of
manufacturing and design. It is the Publisher's desire to present books that
are satisfactory as to their physical qualities and artistic possibilities and
appropriate for their particular use.* THOMAS BOOKS *will be true to those
laws of quality that assure a good name and good will.*

Printed in the United States of America
V-R-1

Library of Congress Cataloging in Publication Data

Valle, Stephen K
    Alcoholism counseling.

    Bibliography: p. 151
    Includes index.
    1. Alcoholism counseling. I. Title.
HV5275.V28   362.2′92   78-23726
ISBN 0-398-03877-5

to my parents

FOREWORD

IN the last twenty years, due to the pioneering efforts of many people, alcoholism has become universally accepted as a disease in the United States. With that acceptance by the many professional societies and disciplines, there has developed a new era in the field of alcoholism treatment and rehabilitation in our time.

Hospitals, slowly but surely, began admitting patients for detoxification and treatment. Doctors, psychiatrists, and psychologists began to change their attitudes and treat an alcoholic person as they would any other patient. It was an awakening that spread like a sunrise across the land and with that awakening, the professionals who had been pioneering the field started to come into their own; no longer was there a feeling of ostracism.

With the battle for funding developing, research became one of the great pioneering areas. Utilization of existing knowledge, and the large and wonderful pool of volunteers, primarily because of Alcoholics Anonymous and Al-Anon, was the natural thing to do. To these few pioneering centers, scientists, and volunteer organizations, we must always be grateful. They were a light in the midst of darkness.

Through three decades of struggle there slowly emerged the trained counselor in the field. From this were spawned training centers to teach the skills and responsibilities of alcoholism counseling. In the beginning, the vast majority of these individuals were themselves recovered alcoholics, sprinkled with a few committed professionals and volunteers. Now the nonalcoholic counselor is common in the field. There has emerged a new and independent profession of alcoholism counseling.

Doctor Stephen K. Valle has made an important contribution to this still-developing profession by writing this book. The author has an excellent background, by training and experience, from which he presents in clear and concise language conclusions that need to be widely read and discussed by those having any interest in this rapidly developing field of public health.

No one doubts the wisdom and validity of alcoholism counseling being a driving force for successful treatment of people with alcohol problems. This work puts in focus many questions, from who can be a counselor, to the problems of credentialing, to ethics and values, and to treatment issues, and even presents a helpful model for alcoholism counselors. It should be an important resource for anyone with an interest in this area of public health.

My congratulations to Doctor Valle for an important contribution to an emerging profession.

HAROLD E. HUGHES
U.S. SENATE, RETIRED

PREFACE

IN March of 1977 I conducted a five-day workshop for the New England Institute of Alcohol Studies on *Alcoholism Counseling: Current Issues and Trends*. The insights and feedback provided by trainees at this and subsequent workshops demonstrated the need for a resource addressing the significant issues confronting alcoholism counseling. In recent years, alcoholism counseling has been moving rapidly from its status as an occupation with uncertain identity to being recognized as a new profession with profound contributions to make to the alcoholism field. However, the emergence of alcoholism counseling as an autonomous profession has been hampered by dissension, infighting, and power struggles. These have a destructive influence upon the profession and, ultimately, the clients.

The major impetus behind this book is the recognition that alcoholism counselors are the driving force behind successful treatment of people with alcohol problems. If their contribution is to have maximum impact, there needs to be a unity of purpose that transcends those issues that tear down rather than build up. This book is an attempt at building. By exploring several issues that are of concern to both the profession and the practitioner, it is hoped that alcoholism counseling will emerge as a profession confident in its purpose, its competence, and its integrity.

I have been continually impressed by the dedication, zeal, and willingness to learn of alcoholism counselors. Perhaps because my involvement in the alcoholism field began as a counselor, I am acutely aware of the difficult task confronting alcoholism counselors and the limited support and recognition they receive. Alcoholism counselors carry the major burden for helping those troubled by alcohol. They feel the alcoholic's pain, helplessness, and remorse, some through their own experience and others because they have permitted themselves to be vulnerable to another person's humanity. Alcoholism counselors are the key to this country's progress in treating our number one drug problem.

While my reaction to the accomplishments of alcoholism counselors is one of respect and awe, I am distressed when I see what little recognition they receive for the services they provide. Because a counselor may not be degreed or may not have developed his or her expertise through the traditional educational and training modalities, he or she is often regarded as something less than a professional. This distortion of reality is a disservice to the counselor, the public, and the consumer.

Alcoholism counselors are professionals by the nature of the functions they perform, and alcoholism counseling is a profession by virtue of its mission, impact, and commitment. This is the premise upon which this book is based. I have attempted to address those issues that are of imminent relevance to the profession of alcoholism counseling and its practitioners. The issues presented here are not at all intended to be comprehensive, but, rather, they are those that most frequently have surfaced as relevant concerns at alcoholism workshops, meetings, and in supervision. They are intended to stimulate communication and action on the part of those committed to the establishment of alcoholism counseling as an autonomous profession.

S.K.V.

ACKNOWLEDGMENTS

THERE are many people who have contributed to the development of this work whom I would like to acknowledge. Foremost, I am grateful to the many trainees of various counseling workshops I have conducted for their openness, encouragement, and feedback which have been both professionally and personally rewarding.

A person's work is a reflection of his training. In this regard, I wish to extend my gratitude to Doctors Bill Anthony, Bob Marinelli, Bob Lasky, and Art Dell Orto, all of Boston University, for contributing to the development of my skills as a helper, researcher, and program developer. I also acknowledge the contribution of Doctor Robert R. Carkhuff and Associates of the Carkhuff Institute of Human Technology, Amherst, Massachusetts. Their consistent modeling of effective helping and living has always challenged me to expand my potential for constructively influencing my world.

I am also grateful to my colleagues and friends at Mount Pleasant Hospital, Lynn, Massachusetts, Doctors Hospital, Worcester, Massachusetts, and American International Health Services for their support and encouragement. Most notably, I wish to acknowledge Mr. Maurice Shear, whose inspirational leadership in alcoholism treatment has been a motivating force of unparalleled significance to me personally and to the alcoholism field. Also, in a deep and special way, I extend my gratitude to my good friend Senator Harold E. Hughes, who, by example, has taught me so much about unselfish helping.

To my friends and colleagues at the Taunton (Massachusetts) Council on Alcoholism, the Taunton Substance Abuse Commission, and the Cape Counseling Center, I extend my appreciation for the part they had in my professional growth and development. In particular, I wish to acknowledge Manny

Lopes, from whom I have learned the most about alcoholism, and Art Thurber, who profoundly facilitated my growth as a clinician.

This product would not have been a reality if it were not for the assistance provided by Mary Valle, Gail Farrand, and Patrice Muchowski. The perspectives and insights provided by Patrice Muchowski have always served as a stimulus for professional excellence. I am deeply grateful to Gail Farrand for the many tedious hours involved in editing, typing, and organizing this manuscript. Her sense of humor, forthright criticism, and gentle persuasion helped to keep me on schedule and to maintain a healthy perspective on this work. Most of all, I am extremely thankful to Mary Valle for her constant patience, unselfishness, and encouragement. Her editorial assistance was invaluable and her understanding and support unwavering.

S.K.V.

CONTENTS

Page

Foreword vii

Preface ix

Acknowledgments xi

Section I
ISSUES FOR THE PROFESSION

Chapter

INTRODUCTION 5

1. TOWARD A PROFESSION OF ALCOHOLISM COUNSELING 7

2. CREDENTIALING 14

3. WHO CAN BE AN ALCOHOLISM COUNSELOR 29

4. A HELPING MODEL FOR ALCOHOLISM COUNSELORS 38

5. CONSUMERISM IN COUNSELING 46

Section II
ISSUES FOR THE PRACTITIONER

INTRODUCTION 59

6. BURN-OUT: AN OCCUPATIONAL HAZARD FOR COUNSELORS .. 61

7. ETHICS AND VALUES IN COUNSELING 75

8. OBSTACLES TO EFFECTIVE COUNSELING.................. 92

9. SUPERVISION 109

10. SIGNIFICANT TREATMENT ISSUES 126

EPILOGUE 149

Bibliography 151

Index 157

Alcoholism Counseling

Section I

ISSUES FOR THE PROFESSION

INTRODUCTION

HISTORICAL developments, responsiveness to contemporary needs, and ability to adapt to future challenges are all elements involved in the emergence of an autonomous profession. This section focuses on these elements from various perspectives. The purpose is to demonstrate the validity of alcoholism counseling as an independent profession which merits the respect and confidence of the public and to challenge the members of this profession to pursue its growth with zeal, integrity, and an unwavering sense of commitment.

Chapter 1 presents a historical perspective on the development of a profession. It also suggests several steps which may be taken to solidify recognition of alcoholism counseling as an autonomous profession. Chapter 2 offers an overview of credentialing as a contemporary need and discusses some of the relevant issues surrounding this topic. The third chapter attempts to provide a constructive perspective of who can be an alcoholism counselor, an emotional and controversial subject in the alcoholism field. Recent research is drawn upon which suggests that specific helping skills are the most important criteria in determining the qualification of a counselor. The fourth chapter presents a helping model that is based upon solid outcome research and is applicable to alcoholism counseling. The last chapter in this section, Consumerism in Counseling, discusses the use of consumers in alcoholism services. It challenges the profession to respond to a contemporary development that is likely to have an impact upon the nature and scope of alcoholism services in the future.

Chapter 1

TOWARD A PROFESSION OF ALCOHOLISM COUNSELING

$\mathbf{A}$ CURRENT stream of thought in the alcoholism field takes the position that there is no need for a separate profession of alcoholism counselors. People holding to this view generally feel the roles and functions of alcoholism counselors can easily be subsumed under the broad category of existing professions rather than emerge as a profession in its own right. Instead of adding to the burgeoning maze of helping professions, this view contends that more would be accomplished by channeling energies in the direction of advocacy for alcoholism services in general or by aligning one's professional identity with an existing helping profession.

While this view is held by many in the field, its advocates are usually those who have already attained the security of professional identity with one of the existing helping professions, i.e. counseling, social work, psychology, etc. The position of this book is that such views represent a denial of the unique contributions of alcoholism counselors and are not valid in view of the historical and contemporary realities of who have been the most potent helpers for people with alcohol problems. Alcoholism counselors are a vital source of manpower who for too long have been given secondary status by alcoholism decision-makers. They are the "front line" force who carry the major responsibility of motivating the troubled, and often reluctant, alcoholic to get help. They carry the brunt of the emotional strain involved in helping an alcoholic and serve as the primary force responsible for coordinating intervention strategies for families and other human service systems. It is the alcoholism counselor who often receives the uninvited phone calls by desperate family members and who must deal firsthand with the antagonism and ambivalence of the community.

The alcoholism counselor is the primary caregiver and the one most responsible for client outcome. Administrators may enable services to emerge and continue, medical personnel may treat the medical problems associated with alcoholism, psychologists may evaluate and treat the emotional difficulties involved with the illness, social workers may provide necessary case management and related services, educators may disseminate and teach necessary information, but it is the counselor who often is the key person responsible for tying all the pieces together and making these resources work for the alcoholic. The purpose is not to diminish the valuable role each service component plays in the alcoholism network, but merely to "tell it like it is." The weight of responsibility for helping the alcoholic is shared by many, but it is the alcoholism counselor who carries the largest portion.

Because alcoholism counselors perform such a vital role in the overall treatment of alcoholism, it is essential that the steps involved in alcoholism counseling becoming a profession in its own right be diligently pursued. Historically (Staub & Kent, 1973) and empirically (Valle, 1976), alcoholism counselors have demonstrated that they provide significant services and can function at levels commensurate with other professionals. There are, however, several issues that need to be considered in the development of a profession of which alcoholism counselors should be thoroughly aware when embarking on such an endeavor. Some of these issues will be addressed in the following paragraphs, but there is one major rationale for the emergence of a new profession of alcoholism counselors that transcends all others: Alcoholism counselors, more than any other treatment-team personnel, experience the highest degree of contact with the alcoholic and witness most directly the suffering associated with alcoholism. This places the counselor in a position of acutely knowing the needs of the alcoholic and being able to identify gaps in the network of alcoholism services. Such a role carries with it immense responsibility. Alcoholism counselors are in a position to constructively influence the quality of services to alcoholics by virtue of their responsibilities and their numbers. There is a unique potential in the

advocacy for improved services, heightened community awareness, and legislative impact within the ranks of alcoholism
counselors that can substantively affect the nature of policies
and priorities in the alcoholism field. The primary motivation
for the emergence of a new profession of alcoholism counselors
must be based upon a firm commitment to improve the quality
of services to those directly and indirectly affected by alcoholism.

CHARACTERISTICS OF A PROFESSION

In considering the essence of a profession, it is important to
examine the motives that stimulate an occupation's movement
toward professionalism. It has already been mentioned that the
primary motivation for the development of a profession of
alcoholism counselors must be to improve the quality of services to alcoholics and their significant others. Any other foundation will serve only to create another group of self-serving
"professionals" who hover together for purposes of self-
protection and self-enhancement. There are enough of these
professional organizations in existence. We do not need another
one!

It is incumbent upon alcoholism counselors to look inward
and examine their own motives for wanting to professionalize
the occupation of alcoholism counseling. If a counselor can
emerge from such a period of self-inventory confirmed in
his/her own mind that the primary reason for developing a
profession is to constructively influence the nature and quality
of services to alcoholics, then he/she is prepared to take the
next step and begin to identify other motives for professionalism. To permit oneself to view the primary motivation mentioned above as the sole motivation for professionalism is both
naive and delusive. There are several other motives which need
to be identified and brought to awareness. These, however, are
secondary, and, while recognized as powerful motivators, they
must always be subjugated to the primary.

In addition to providing a means for promoting client welfare, the motives for professionalization may also include in-

creasing the social status of those within the profession, raising income levels, increasing power and prestige, gaining more control over services and resources, and establishing role autonomy. It may also be argued that professionalization can result in increased counselor effectiveness and efficiency by (a) excluding incompetent persons, (b) having more influence on decision-makers, such as legislators and community policy-makers, and (c) having a greater impact on the attitudes and behaviors of other professionals who may help or harm alcoholic clients (Solomone, 1972). Thus motivation for developing a profession may encompass such issues as job security, status, power, job autonomy, and prestige, as well as concern for quality services.

The nature of a profession is the existence of a body of knowledge and skills within which its members profess to be skilled and to which they subscribe (Hughes, 1963). A profession also separates itself from the well-meaning neighbor or amateur by virtue of its mission, the knowledge and skills possessed by its members, and the training it requires its members to complete before admission to the profession is permitted. It is also characteristic of a profession to view itself as having the prerogative of defining what services are within the mandate of the profession and how they are to be delivered. Another characteristic of a profession is that it expects its members to maintain a balance between interest and detachment (Hughes, 1963). Objectivity in the performance of one's profession is expected as is a concern for the larger, more universal issues confronting a profession. Professions also have a set of acceptable and unacceptable standards for behavior with a means for monitoring its members in relation to these standards. Moore (1970) has stressed the importance of organization as an important step in professionalization as well as personal autonomy in the performance of one's professional duties.

A review of the literature on professions identifies certain traits that appear to be characteristic of successful professions. Identified from these have been traits that are relevant to alcoholism counseling. These are listed below to serve as a point of reference for alcoholism counselors to evaluate their position in relation to these points. Suggested characteristics that would serve to identify the profession of alcoholism counseling include the following:

1. A common mission that is service-oriented to which its members share a solidarity of commitment.
2. A unique body of knowledge and skills to which its members subscribe.
3. A system for self-regulation through a code of ethics that serves to define and maintain acceptable standards of behavior.
4. An indentifiable system of educating, training, and/or experience that provides the criteria for entrance into the profession as well as defining standards for maintaining and upgrading one's skills and knowledge.
5. A uniform mechanism for credentialing that clearly identifies those who possess the necessary training, knowledge, and skills to function legitimately as members in good standing of the profession.
6. A unified organization that serves as a spokesman for the profession and as an advocate for its causes.
7. A clear definition of one's role that allows for professional autonomy in the performance of one's duties.

An assessment of these points in terms of where alcoholism counseling is currently functioning yields mixed results. Most alcoholism professionals would agree that there is a high level of commitment and dedication among the ranks of alcoholism counselors. They receive little recognition for their services, are accorded a low status by other professionals, receive minimal compensation for their services, and enjoy limited job autonomy. Most people would be driven from the field under such conditions, but alcoholism counselors' reservoir of dedication for helping alcoholics has historically overridden these other concerns. There is not, however, an identifiable body of knowledge unique to alcoholism counseling, nor are there unique skills to which counselors can subscribe. These certainly exist, but they have not been uniformly identified, accepted, or disseminated by the field in general. One of the primary tasks that lies ahead for the profession of alcoholism counseling is the concrete identification of its role, its function, and its theoretical basis for existence. It is also necessary for alcoholism counselors to develop a uniform code of ethics that defines acceptable behavior for its members and insures protection for the public from incompetent practitioners.

Reviewing the historical developments of other health care professions reveals a relationship between federal support for training of personnel and the emergence of that profession. Such a relationship in the alcoholism field is difficult to find when the priorities of federal funding for alcoholism are examined. Training has received only limited support in terms of programmatic priorities and allocated funds, despite the reality that effective programs require effectively trained people. If alcoholism counseling is to emerge as a potent force in the delivery of alcoholism services, resources that enable entry-level counselors and current counselors to obtain training must receive more substantial support. A training strategy linked to a career concept ladder for alcoholism counselors is vital to the profession of alcoholism counseling. Evidence demonstrating the impact of training does exist (Valle & Anthony, 1977; Rosenberg, 1975; Rosenberg et al., 1976). A national system identifying training needs, resources, and technologies, as well as mechanisms, to permit alcoholism counselors to be trained is desperately needed.

Closely related to the issue of training is the need for a uniform system of credentialing alcoholism counselors. While steps have been taken by private organizations and government endorsed and/or sponsored groups, there has yet to emerge a national system specifying the criteria and process for becoming recognized as an alcoholism counselor. The lack of such a system is a disservice to the public and serves to perpetuate the myth that alcoholism counselors are somewhat less than professional. A national credentialing system is an absolute necessity if the occupation of alcoholism counseling is to emerge as a profession! (Most authors cringe at the thought of their statements becoming out of date. It would, however, delight this author if the above statements on credentialing were to become obsolete.)

In addition to the need for action in the above areas, alcoholism counseling requires a unified organization that advocates the profession's goals and objectives. Currently there are several organizations and groups vying for the loyalty of alcoholism counselors. Some of these are national in scope, while others are statewide or local in nature. This tends to have a fragmenting effect on a profession as potentially common goals often become diluted and obscured. One national organization devoted solely to professional issues of alcoholism counseling is needed. Such an organization, united in purpose and strong in numbers, can dramatically affect the pace at which alcoholism counseling becomes recognized as a profession.

Accepted professions have a means for communicating knowledge and information regarding the development of their profession. This is most often accomplished through professional publications. The establishment of a specific journal for alcoholism counselors which reports on recent developments in the area of counselor theory, practice, and research should be achieved. Such a publication would provide a forum for consideration of relevant issues and encourage counselors to maintain their growth as professionals.

The final characteristic suggested for a profession of alcoholism counseling relates to the role of the counselor and the need to define that role. Currently there exists a vague concept of the alcoholism counselor's role, and this varies, depending upon the setting. Job autonomy cannot be experienced when employers have mixed conceptions of what an alcoholism counselor does or should do, nor can it be realized when the counselor himself is uncertain of his role. Job autonomy that stems from a concrete conception of what it is one does and is competent to do is a trademark of a professional. Alcoholism counseling has yet to establish such a basis for functioning.

The preceding steps toward becoming a profession are offered as guidelines to solidify the recognition of alcoholism counseling as a viable profession. Accomplishing these steps will serve to stimulate growth of the profession and to enhance its recognition by the public and other professionals.

Chapter 2

CREDENTIALING

ONE of the central criteria in the process toward recognition of alcoholism counseling as an established profession is the development of a mechanism that requires certain standards of excellence in the preparation and performance of its members. Occupations that have attained the status of a profession have in common a means by which they can assure the public that their members are adequately trained and in possession of the requisite knowledge and skills to competently render the services requested. Perhaps no issues are more critical to the emergence of alcoholism counseling as a profession than the issues of credentialing for counselors and the credentialing of training programs that prepare counselors to perform their duties. Without a system for recognizing alcoholism counselors as individuals competent to deliver services, and without a system for assuring the quality of training that a counselor receives in preparation for his or her role, there will be little, if any, acceptance of alcoholism counseling as a profession. This chapter will explore the credentialing of individual counselors and the credentialing of counselor training programs, as they are complementary concerns to the overall issue of professionalism in alcoholism counseling.

PERSPECTIVES ON CREDENTIALING
ALCOHOLISM COUNSELORS

There has been a general assumption in the health field that credentialing of those who deliver services is necessary to protect the consumer from incompetent and unethical practices. This has resulted in a proliferation of professional organizations, legal statutes, and standard-setting bodies that protect the public and professions from unscrupulous practitioners who cause harm to patients. The credentialing of alcoholism counselors has emerged as a vital issue for these reasons and others as well. As alcoholism services become integrated into the mainstream of health care in this country, the issue of third-party reimbursement becomes increasingly critical. If historical precedent can be viewed as a valid indicator of future action, reimbursement for the services of alcoholism counselors will be contingent upon a system that recognizes those counselors qualified to provide counseling services to alcoholics. Credentialing of alcoholism counselors would provide recognition to counselors for their valuable services, serve as an impetus to the acceptance of alcoholism counselors as peers by other health care providers, and help to assure quality care to alcoholic persons and their families.

While on the surface there appears to be a general recognition that credentialing alcoholism counselors could only be an asset and should be pursued vigorously, there are several problems inherent in the issue that need to be examined. Such problems emerge when one attempts to define what is meant by credentialing and how it translates to the field of alcoholism counseling. The unabridged edition of the *Random House Dictionary* defines a credential as "anything that provides the basis for confidence, belief, credit, etc." It would follow, then, that in order for a credential to have meaning, there must be a common understanding of the functions of an alcoholism counselor. Unfortunately, there has not been a standardized definition of the exact functions of an alcoholism counselor that distinguishes it from the functions of other counselors. Is it a knowledge base about alcoholism that distinguishes the alcoholism counselor from a social worker? Are the therapeutic skills of an alcoholism counselor uniquely different from the therapeutic skills of clinicians from other professions? What are the professional functions of an alcoholism counselor, and how are they distinguished from the functions of correctional counselors, marriage and family counselors, rehabilitation counselors, drug abuse counselors, guidance counselors, and other helping professionals who provide counseling services? In order for a credential to have meaning, there needs to be a consensus from the field of what it is an alcoholism counselor does, what his/her role is, and what skills and knowledge he/she must possess in order to function effectively. A credentialing process that is not based upon a clarification of such issues will run the risk of perpetuating rather than resolving problems of professional identity.

In a profession there are several means of credentialing. It is important for counselors to be able to define who they are and what their function is. It is also important to have an understanding of the different types of credentialing a profession may choose to adopt. The most common forms of credentialing for professions are registration, certification, licensure, and accreditation. Registration is usually a procedure that involves a formal listing of persons who have met certain minimum qualifications. Requirements for registration are generally so minimal that there is not much status attached to simply being registered. It tends to serve as a means of identifying professional associations and affiliations rather than differentiating between competence and incompetence. Certification, on the other hand, recognizes the competence of individuals by officially authorizing them to use the title prescribed by the profession (Forster, 1977). It is most often granted by professional associations and includes a voluntary standard-setting process that serves to identify those who meet prescribed standards. Certification can also be awarded by voluntary associations, agencies, or governmental bodies, as is done in the certification of school counselors and teachers. The requirements for certification are more demanding than for registration and generally utilize criteria based upon education and training, supervised experience, and performance by examination, thus lending significant status or prestige to the profession. The field of alcoholism counseling appears to be directing its major efforts toward the certification of its counselors.

Licensure is a process used by governments to regulate the practice and title of a profession. Generally authorized by legislation, it subjects violators to greater legal sanctions than does certification (Forster, 1977). Licensure is most desirable when the majority of the profession is involved in private practice, one example being the inclusion of legislation regulating the use of the title and the practice of physicians and psychologists.

Whereas the above credentialing processes refer to individuals, accreditation is the recognition given an agency or institution for the maintenance of specific levels of excellence verified through initial and periodic evaluations. Just as accreditation of treatment facilities assures the consumer that certain established qualifications have been met by a facility, accreditation of training programs assures counselors that a training program meets acceptable standards that can minimally be expected to assure quality training.

Vagueness and confusion of identity resulting from overlapping with other professions is another area of concern in the credentialing of alcoholism counselors. Alcoholism counselors often serve the same clients that psychiatrists, social workers, and other professionals serve, making it difficult for the public to distinguish between alcoholism counselors and those trained in other helping disciplines. Since they all draw heavily upon related theory and methods of the behavioral sciences, there appears to be an overlapping of professions. However, other disciplines have established their identities as independent professions and are recognized by the public as such. Credentialing can be an opportunity for the profession of alcoholism counseling to demonstrate its uniqueness among the helping professions, if the standards are linked to the actual knowledge, skills, and attitudes alcoholism counselors require in order to be effective. If alcoholism counselors cannot identify and articulate their unique professional competencies, then the public is likely to wonder if alcoholism counseling is indeed a separate profession or just an appendage of other existing human service professions.

One of the critical issues in the credentialing of health professionals is having a recognized credential does not guarantee competency. There are those who feel strongly that credentialing has failed to protect the public and has been more successful in protecting professionals (Gross, 1977). While supposing to answer the problem of delivering quality service to the public, the credentialing scene in America, particularly in the health care professions, has raised some serious questions. How does one differentiate between the competent and

incompetent? Who decides what is acceptable professional behavior and what is not? How are these decision-makers chosen?
What are considered to be the competencies of a professional
and how are these measured? The failure of existing professions
to adequately answer these questions has led many to doubt the
legitimacy of the credentialing process. Let us hope that this
profession, in its effort to certify alcoholism counselors, will
not follow the path of other professions and be subject to similar questions that are being posed with increasing frequency.
For example, Gross (1977) asserts that licensing is misleading
in that it promises to work in the public interest but instead
actually maintains the interests of exclusive clubs against those
of the public. Credentialing organizations have tended to grow
into rigid bureaucracies that give little or no attention to therapist effectiveness or training (Rogers, 1973). Arbuckle (1977)
explains that if a credentialing procedure such as licensure is to
control and measure professional competency, then it is misleading, because it actually permits a person to use a certain
title but does not license one to perform certain services. The
result is that often the incompetent practitioner changes his or
her title. Because most credentialing processes are not based
upon specific competencies, there is the danger of excluding
the competent nondegreed therapist who may have the skills
but not the formal piece of paper. Such practices serve to create
"a mystique that hides the unskilled but licensed and victimizes
the skilled but unlicensed" (Gross, 1977). Moreover, the
exclusive-club mentality spurred on by the credentialing band-
wagon has often led professionals to neglect national manpower shortages, to hinder the opportunity for members of
minority groups to enter the profession, and often to ignore the
contributions of those who are willing to do what many professionals appear uninterested in doing, such as serving the poor,
the aged, and the minorities (Roemer, 1974; Rogers, 1973;
Shimberg, 1972).

If alcoholism counseling is to have an impact as a unique
profession, there must be more creativity and foresight demonstrated in its credentialing process. No criteria speaks more for
a profession than its means for regulating its members. As we

move in the direction of credentialing alcoholism counselors, we must do more than imitate other professions.

RECENT DEVELOPMENTS IN CREDENTIALING COUNSELORS

There are three recent developments related to credentialing that will be discussed in order to add to our perspective on the issue of credentialing alcoholism counselors. Of late there have been increased efforts to credential other helping professionals who perform functions similar to those of alcoholism counselors. The movement to credential professional counselors will be briefly discussed because of the implications for alcoholism counseling. In addition, the Public Health Service of the U.S. Department of Health, Education and Welfare has made recommendations regarding the credentialing of health manpower in general. These recommendations, along with those of the National Institute of Alcohol Abuse and Alcoholism's planning panel on alcoholism counselor credentialing, will also be considered.

In most states it is becoming standard procedure to regulate the practice of counseling and psychotherapy, either through licensure or certification. Currently forty-nine states have some form of legislation regarding the practice of psychology; however, many counselors with professional training in psychology have encountered resistance in their attempt to gain recognition because of certain restrictions in the legal statutes or from a narrow interpretation of legislation by the respective state boards. Consequently, the licensure or certification of counselors has emerged as a major professional issue. The American Personnel and Guidance Association, the country's largest counseling association (more than 40,000 members), has adopted a position in favor of licensure for professional counselors (APGA, 1975). While at present only a few states have enacted a professional counselor licensure law, many have indicated a desire for such legislation. The APGA Commission on Licensure has recently (1976-1977) undertaken a study on National Recognition and Identification of Professional Counselors. This is an indication that credentialing for professional counselors is imminent.

Several complex problems surround these developments. For example, many counselors contend that counseling is a unique mental health profession, and although there is overlap with psychology, they feel counselors should be regulated by legislation unique to counseling. Others maintain that the differences between counseling and psychology are minor and object to licensure laws that restrict counselors from practicing their profession. Many heated debates have occurred between professional organizations with some issues being left to the courts to resolve, i.e. *Weldon v. Virginia State Board of Psychologist Examiners* (1974). A narrow interpretation of psychology demonstrated by some psychology boards has caused counselors with psychological training to unite in an effort to protect their right to practice their profession. While it remains to be seen whether credentialing of professional counselors will follow the same trend as psychology boards, there are implications for alcoholism counselors that need to be examined. If credentialing of professional counselors follows the trend established in states that already have legislation regulating the practice of counseling, counselors would be required to meet certain standards. For example, some states require professional counselors to hold a master's degree in counseling or personnel services, to have four years of counseling experience, two years of post-degree supervised experience, and also to pass an examination. Many alcoholism counselors would not meet these requirements, but if this becomes the accepted criteria for recognition as a professional counselor, what does that mean to alcoholism counselors? If alcoholism counselors cannot be credentialed as professional counselors, what are they? The designation of anything less than professional, such as subprofessional or paraprofessional, would hardly give impetus to the emergence of alcoholism counseling as a profession. The danger in the movement to credential professional counselors is the exclusion from its ranks of those helpers who provide competent services but who do not hold formal degrees. This would represent a disservice to the alcoholic who cares very little if the counselor has a degree or not. What matters most is whether or not a counselor has the skills to effect constructive change and whether he or she can effectively help an alcoholic to recover. The urgency for alcoholism professionals to respond to and resolve this issue cannot be overstated.

Another implication of these recent developments is that third-party reimbursement, a major impetus to the credentialing movement in alcoholism, may be influenced by the trend to credential professional counselors. Psychologists have already attained access to most third-party reimbursement mechanisms. Credentialed professional counselors are in the process of attaining similar recognition and, in fact, have been recognized by some carriers for such specialty services as marriage counseling. Will third-party payers reimburse for services provided by counselors who do not meet the standards of credentialed professional counselors? Whether or not the movement to credential alcoholism counselors can be independent from the movement to credential professional counselors is a question that merits thorough consideration by the field.

There are also some nonlegislative developments relating to credentialing counselors that are worth mentioning. Currently, there are at least four models for national credentialing that exist through which counselors can receive some form of credentialing without state or federal legislation (Sweeney & Witmer, 1977). One example is the American Association of Marriage and Family Counselors that has established educational, experience, and supervision requirements in order to be recognized as a clinical member. Rehabilitation counselors have established a national certification process that has similar requirements but also draws upon the results of an examination and peer evaluations as criteria for certification. The Commission on Rehabilitation Counselor Certification also provides for accreditation of counselor training programs. Two other professional associations which have operating models for credentialing counselors are the American Association of Sex Educators and Counselors and the International Transactional Analysis Association, both of which have established certification criteria.

Another form of national credentialing has been proposed by

the Department of Health, Education and Welfare (U.S. Dept. H.E.W., 1977). This proposal evolved from a series of departmental and Public Health Service statements concerning the problems caused by the proliferation of licensed health occupations. After terminating a moratorium on new legislation to license health occupations, the Public Health Service issued a report with recommendations for improving the licensure and certification of health personnel, including counselors. Their recommendations include the creation of a national certification commission which would develop and evaluate criteria for recognizing certification organizations, provide consultation and technical assistance to certification organizations, and participate in the development of national standards for the credentialing of selected health occupations. The report also recommended that states exercise caution before enacting any new legislation that would license additional categories of health manpower. It also included recommendations to improve current licensure procedures and encourage credentialing bodies to promote competency measures to determine the qualifications of health personnel and to assure their continued competence.

These recommendations are significant because they represent the position of the federal government, the impact of which is likely to filter down to all credentialing organizations as well as to affect positions taken by insurance carriers. In 1975, when the moratorium on licensure activities was lifted by H.E.W., the National Institute on Alcohol Abuse and Alcoholism responded to the need for credentialing alcoholism counselors by establishing a planning panel to explore this issue. This panel concluded that the credentialing of alcoholism personnel would fulfill three basic needs:

1. Assure the quality of health care provided the alcoholic patient by treatment personnel.
2. Achieve recognition of alcoholism treatment personnel as health professionals.
3. Provide for a mechanism by which third-party payers could compensate personnel or facilities for services rendered the alcoholic patient with an assurance that quality

care was being rendered (NIAAA, 1977).

The planning panel also recommended that the specific requirements for credentialing be left to an independent organization comprised of various representatives from the alcoholism field. With the establishment of the National Commission for Credentialing Alcoholism Counselors, such issues as the type of credential, the skills and competencies required of alcoholism counselors, how these competencies will be measured, what relationship credentialed alcoholism counselors will have to other credentialed health professionals, along with other issues that have been raised in this chapter, will hopefully be clarified. Given the demand for recognition from within the field, public pressure for quality care, and recent developments in credentialing health care personnel, one can be assured that credentialing of alcoholism counselors is on its way. The challenge before the profession is to decide whether the credentialing effort actually reflects the realities of the field in a creative and imaginative manner or simply becomes a rubber stamp of other professions' weaknesses.

ACCREDITATION OF TRAINING PROGRAMS

Credentialing of alcoholism counselors cannot realistically be viewed independently from the training process which prepares counselors for their roles. If credentialing is to function as a mechanism by which the public can be assured of quality care from those who use the title of alcoholism counselor, then there needs to be a direct link between the training process and the individual credentialing of counselors. Training programs need to assure the public and the consumer that the services they deliver maintain certain acceptable standards. Accreditation is the credentialing term most commonly used to denote an educational or training program which meets acceptable professional standards. Thus, accreditation attests to the fact that a program, facility, or institution has met certain acceptable standards to ensure quality of service, while certification, registration, or licensure is used to recognize an individual's legitimacy as a professional.

There are a diversity of training workshops, schools, seminars, and programs that offer alcoholism counselors an opportunity to develop their skills. As the counselor is provided with more training alternatives, it becomes incumbent upon the profession to develop some means of assuring counselors that acceptable standards of excellence are being met in the delivery of training services. In this regard, a major step has been taken by the Eastern Area Alcohol Education and Training Program, Inc., in response to the needs expressed by counselors, training programs, credentialing bodies, counselor associations, and administrators of treatment programs. The E.A.A.E.T.P. has developed accreditation standards for alcoholism counselor training programs and has formed an accreditation council whose function is to implement, manage, and regulate the accreditation standards.

The accreditation standards for alcoholism counselor training programs, developed by the E.A.A.E.T.P., represent a major step in the credentialing process because the level of counselor functioning is directly related to the quality of training received. These standards were developed with wide input from the field and were thoroughly field-tested to ensure their relevancy. A manual (E.A.A.E.T.P., 1977) describing the steps that training programs can take to become accredited and the specific standards that must be met has been prepared by E.A.A.E.T.P. and is available on request. A general overview of the accreditation process and the standards will be presented to familiarize readers with the accreditation standards and to gain insight into this important development.

The accreditation standards developed by the E.A.A.E.T.P. are based upon certain fundamental principles. These principles reflect the philosophical base from which the accreditation standards emerged. They state that the primary purpose of all training programs is essentially to assure that quality services are provided to alcoholic individuals, that certain human and legal rights be respected at all times, that a competent and ethical training staff be assured, that training programs be responsive to the community, and that programs have clearly defined goals and objectives. The specific standards are divided into three major categories: policies and procedures, methodology, and content. The policies and procedures section delineates requirements that programs must meet in the areas of program administration and management, admission criteria and procedures, faculty qualifications, program crediting, and program evaluation. The methodology section specifies requirements for program intensity and methods. The content section outlines the knowledge areas that should be covered, including information on alcohol and alcoholism, helping issues, assessment and evaluation, case management, and treatment skills.

The accreditation standards were developed in light of the variety of training alternatives present in the field with the intent of maintaining quality while being sensitive to the need for flexibility. The E.A.A.E.T.P. accreditation council has also developed a survey and review process involving a system for program self-study, evaluation of the program by specialists, and a periodic review process to determine if a program continues to meet the standards. Training programs are encouraged to involve themselves in the accreditation process as a means of demonstrating their credibility as well as to give impetus to the emerging profession of alcoholism counselors.

The credentialing of training programs through accreditation and the credentialing of individual counselors through certification (or other means) cannot be regarded as separate entities if alcoholism counseling is to establish itself as an autonomous and unique profession. It is important to the profession that they be linked and that this linkage be based upon a responsiveness to the field. The precedent already set by other professions is that credentialing efforts were originally based upon a motivation for quality, but gradually changed to one of self-interest and elitism. Alcoholism counseling as a profession must avoid this pattern if it is to have a constructive impact.

ISSUES

Since credentialing of alcoholism counselors and counselor training programs is an inevitable step in the growth towards a profession, great care needs to be taken to ensure that the process is beneficial and constructive. While there is much to learn from other professions that have developed along similar lines, we should not blindly copy them. Similarities and overlap do exist with such other professions as social work, psychology, and counseling; however, we must not forget that alcoholism counseling is unique in several aspects. Its heritage is different from other professions, and much of the knowledge, skills, and attitudes needed to be an effective alcoholism counselor are specific to working with the alcoholic and his/her family. The training needs and technologies also differ from traditional training programs of other professions. Such distinctions need to be attended to in earnest if credentialing in alcoholism counseling and training is to be meaningful. Some perspectives to consider are as follows:

1. The most feasible form of credentialing for individual counselors is certification. It carries significant prestige without being burdened with the complexities and political maneuvering that often accompany licensing regulations. Certification on a national basis is preferable to fifty separate sets of certification standards due to the fact that reciprocity between states and recognition by third-party payers and other professional associations would be less cumbersome. A national registry of alcoholism counselors should be developed and continually updated to provide an accurate reference resource for interested parties.

2. If certification is to be meaningful, it must be directly related to the professional functions of the individual to be certified. Global standards that simply reflect certain education, training, or experience requirements testify to a process that assumes certain competencies and skills. The experience of other professions and the research literature on counselor education and training demonstrate that this assumption is not valid. Certification standards should be reflective of counselor functions and skills and competencies necessary to perform these functions. It should also be directly related to the evaluation of the degree of achievement of these competencies.

3. The question of who determines the requirements and procedures for counselor credentialing is a critical issue. The selection of commission members must be carefully done to ensure that the field is adequately represented. The danger for commissions or boards that have significant influence over the development of a profession is that they can become as political as they are professional. Direct access to the decision-making process in the selection of commission members must be given to consumers and representative alcoholism groups in order to keep the process a professional rather than a political one.

4. The functions of the credentialing bodies and the tenure of its members must be clearly defined. Every effort should be made to avoid the tendency to form "in-groups" that perpetuate personal or professional bias. Limiting the tenure of its members and establishing a mechanism that requires continued review and updating of standards will help in this regard. If the credentialing board is to be contributory to the profession of alcoholism counseling, care needs to be taken to ensure that requirements reflect what is, rather than what was. Historically, credentialing boards have not been the leaders in the advancement of the profession. This precedent ought not to be followed if alcoholism counseling is to make its mark as a profession with substantive contribution.

5. If credentialing of individual counselors is to mean anything, it must be inherently related to the programs that train and educate the individual to be credentialed. Standards for individual counselors must be an extension of what is learned in the educational and training programs. There should be also a relevant extension of these processes to the employer. Credentialing of both individuals and training programs is of little value if what is learned and practiced does not relate to what employers regard as needed for effective performance. If it is to be successful, credentialing cannot exist in a vacuum, distant from the day-to-day realities of the field. A viable credentialing model must include an ongoing relationship and a conti-

nuity between programs that educate and train counselors, the professional organizations that represent counselors, and the facilities that hire counselors.

Chapter 3

WHO CAN BE AN
ALCOHOLISM COUNSELOR

ONE of the unique characteristics of the alcoholism field is the range of backgrounds, training, and experience represented by those who are in helping roles. It is common to find a wide range of people with different training and experience, from physicians to community volunteers, committed to a common goal of helping the person troubled by alcohol.

While there is consensus of purpose among alcoholism helpers, the issue of who can most effectively help the alcoholic is one that clouds the field with controversy and emotionalism. Many feel strongly that only people who are recovering from the illness can fully understand what it is like to be alcoholic and that, therefore, they are most effective in counseling other alcoholics. "I know what it's like because I've been there myself" is often stated as a unique qualification by recovering alcoholic counselors. There are others, however, who feel just as strongly that one must have some professional training in order to be an effective counselor and that the asset of similar experience does not necessarily contribute to counseling effectiveness. People who hold to this view are quick to point out that over-identification with a client may detract from counseling effectiveness and that being recovered may therefore be a disadvantage.

While there are arguments on both sides of the continuum which appear to have merit, positions have tended to be so polarized by emotionalism that it has become difficult to separate the issues from the rhetoric. Unfortunately, the motivation of many alcoholism helpers for providing the highest quality care for the alcoholic is often clouded by the need to establish one's own professional identity and sphere of influence and power.

The subjectivity and emotionalism represented by both those with personal life experience and those without such experience interfere with the ability to recognize the contributions that each has to offer. When the issues of who is qualified to be an alcoholism counselor is raised at alcoholism gatherings, it is most often characterized by an excessive amount of negativism that tends to polarize the field. If the issue of who can be an alcoholism helper is to have a constructive rather than a destructive effect on the field, there needs to be a shift from focusing on deficits to recognizing and enhancing the strengths of each group. There are unique contributions that recovering helpers bring to the helping relationship that need to be identified, and there are contributions a nonalcoholic brings from his/her discipline of professional training that also need to be identified. The challenge for all alcoholism helpers is to suspend one's own opinions, bias, and subjectivity so that energies can be expended on identifying objectively who can best be an alcoholism counselor and what are the skills, knowledge areas, and competencies that constitute an effective alcoholism helper.

The issue of who can be an effective helper is not limited solely to the alcoholism field. As a whole, helping professions have been concerned with the issue of who can most effectively help others, particularly since it became evident that the demand for competent helpers far outweighed the supply. In order to attain a perspective on who can best be an alcoholism counselor, it is important to understand some of the significant developments in human services that have emerged in response to this issue.

THE PARAPROFESSIONAL MOVEMENT

An extensive amount of literature has been produced regarding the utilization of paraprofessional workers in human services (Brown, 1974; Carkhuff, 1969; Delworth et al., 1974; Gartner & Riessman, 1972; Staub & Kent, 1973). The term paraprofessional is difficult to define but, in general, refers to persons who have been given responsibility for performing functions often performed by professionals but who do not have the formal educational backgrounds of most professionals. Though they may not have the same formal credentials as professionals, they have demonstrated a range of capabilities that enable them to perform tasks central to the goals and objectives of helping agencies. That is, they perform professional functions but lack the recognition and status afforded the professional.

While the beginning of the paraprofessional movement was marked by considerable challenge from the ranks of the professionals, it is now widely accepted that persons without formal preparation and traditional credentials can provide significant and beneficial helping services (Gartner & Riessman, 1974). An extensive body of material has been collected from research and practice providing compelling evidence as to the effectiveness of paraprofessional counselors (Brown, 1974; Carkhuff, 1969, 1971; Carkhuff & Truax, 1965; Truax & Lister, 1970; Valle, 1975). The well-designed studies of Carkhuff and his associates concluded that paraprofessionals receiving limited training can be just as effective as professionals in facilitating constructive client change, and that lengthy professional training is not a necessary prerequisite for effective functioning as a therapist (Carkhuff, 1969; Carkhuff & Berenson, 1976). As a result of this and other research, Carkhuff concluded that the terms paraprofessional and professional are inappropriate and advocated the use of the term "functional professional." For the functional professional, the central criteria is how one functions and the skills he/she possesses, rather than degrees resulting from training or criteria based solely on life experience.

The impact of the paraprofessional movement upon human services has been profound. It has made helping and therapeutic services more accessible, more cost-effective, and more accountable. Professionals trained traditionally can no longer afford the luxury of relying on their credentials alone in order to demonstrate their effectiveness. The realization that people with limited training can achieve many of the same results as credentialed helpers has caused many to reconsider the issues regarding utilization of manpower resources in the helping professions.

Although the paraprofessional movement has only recently presented a challenge to the traditional views of most helping professions, alcoholism is unique. Professionals have historically neglected the alcoholic, whereas alcoholism services have relied upon lay people to provide basic helping services. The early Yale Plan alcoholism clinics at Hartford and New Haven, Connecticut, utilized recovering alcoholics, before it was popular, to draw upon paraprofessional resources. The immense pool of people belonging to Alcoholics Anonymous has also been involved in helping other alcoholics for decades and still comprises the most responsive resource for helping another alcoholic. The professional establishment, on the other hand, has a history of benign neglect and questionable effectiveness in its treatment of alcoholic people. Only since the Hughes Act of 1970, which established the National Institute on Alcohol Abuse and Alcoholism, has there been a concerted effort among the ranks of the professionals for the recognition and treatment of alcoholism. A result of these developments is that the alcoholism field currently is comprised of paraprofessionals with a history of personal life experience in dealing with alcoholic people and professionals representing a wide range of formal disciplines. It is no wonder that the issue of who can be an alcoholism helper is a significant one for the field when there exists such a diverse range of training backgrounds and experience by those in the helping roles.

FACILITATIVE DIMENSIONS

Basic to the question of who can be an alcoholism helper is the identification of what constitutes effective helping. Research in counseling and psychotherapy has devoted much of its efforts to the identification of what accounts for constructive helping outcome. Extensive evidence from a variety of researchers has been compiled which concludes that constructive helping outcome is, in part, related to certain skills of the helper (Carkhuff, 1969, 1972; Rogers, 1957). The facilitative conditions necessary to encourage client self-exploration and constructive change have been identified as empathy, genuineness, respect, and concreteness or specificity in communication. Absence or low levels of functioning by helpers on these dimensions result in destructive consequences, while helpers functioning at high levels of these dimensions facilitate constructive change in helpees. Rating scales that measure these characteristics have also been developed and incorporated into a systematic training technology which has been widely utilized throughout the helping professions (Carkhuff, 1969; Carkhuff & Pierce, 1975).

Identification of the facilitative conditions that in part affect constructive change in helpees has been a major breakthrough in the helping professions. It has resulted in the demystification of the helping process, as these skills are not solely the possession of professionally trained people. In addition, it has been found through extensive research that lay people can be trained to develop and function at levels equal to or, in some cases, higher than professionals. There is, in fact, research evidence indicating that students of professional training programs in the helping professions actually graduate at lower levels than when they entered, leaving one to question the efficacy of such training programs (Carkhuff, 1969).

A benefit derived from identifying the relationship between the facilitative conditions and constructive helping outcome is the opening of the helping field to others than those coming from the ranks of traditional helping professions. However, it is important to recognize that while high levels of the facilitative conditions are necessary, they are not of themselves sufficient to account for client change. Carkhuff (1972) and others (Lazarus, 1971) stress the importance of other aspects involved in effective helping which stem from the facilitative conditions. There also are many unknowns yet to be discovered about helping relationships and what constitutes effective helping. Given the realization that research has yet to specify all the ingredients involved in effective helping relationships, there is conclusive research evidence indicating that helpers need to be highly skilled in communicating empathy, respect, genuineness, and concreteness with helpees. These ingredients are necessary and therefore represent an essential foundation for effective helping.

In a study involving a cross section of alcoholism helpers representing a variety of alcohol programs, it was found that the overall functioning of alcoholism workers on these dimensions was below minimally effective levels (Valle & Anthony, 1977). That is, their ability to communicate empathic understanding, respect, genuineness, and concreteness or specificity was below the minimal level needed to engage helpees in meaningful self-exploration. Although the mean level of functioning of alcoholism helpers in this and subsequent studies was found to be below the level previous research indicated was necessary for constructive helping, the level was commensurate with that of helpers from other professional disciplines. Alcoholism helpers and helpers from other professional disciplines were found to be functioning at approximately level 2.0 on a 5 point scale, where level 1.0 indicates a very ineffective level, level 3.0 a minimally effective level, and level 5.0 a very effective level. Thus, on those helper-offered dimensions considered to be, in part, related to effective helping outcome, alcoholism helpers function at levels commensurate with other helping professionals. Considering that the overall level was below the minimally effective level, we are not comforted by the findings that alcoholism helpers are really no different from other helping professionals. There is, however, more to be told.

In this same study, it was found that alcoholism helpers exposed to a relatively brief training period (30 hours) can increase their level of functioning from ineffective to effective levels of helping skills that incorporate the facilitative dimensions. Whereas alcoholism helpers were functioning at around level 2.0 prior to training in the helper dimensions of empathy, respect, genuineness, and concreteness, after training they were found to be functioning at nearly level 4.0 (Valle & Anthony, 1977).

RECOVERING OR DEGREED HELPERS?

At the core of the controversy regarding who is effective in helping the alcoholic is the issue of whether the degreed helper or the nondegreed helper, who also is a recovering alcoholic, is better qualified. One view asserts that helping is a specialized enterprise based upon a thorough understanding and grasp of the behavioral sciences. This view contends that one should have some formal training indicated by a degree from an institution of higher education. The other view contends that helping is a broad human function which can be accomplished effectively by people who have natural ability resulting from dealing constructively with the problem themselves. Rather than the possession of a degree, experience is considered to be the most important criteria. The importance of this debate within the alcoholism field goes beyond the general issue of the professional versus the paraprofessional. For years the only help for the alcoholic person was another alcoholic, and thus resentment is easily generated when recovering alcoholics are told they need more training in order to be effective helpers. Where were the degreed people when there were no jobs in the alcoholism field is a question often asked of professionals who are quick to de-emphasize the value of being recovered.

While there is often a great deal of emotional energy spent on defending either viewpoint, such positions are rarely based upon factual data. Assumptions, opinions, and "gut feelings" tend to dominate both sides with little effort generated toward obtaining objective information. This condition provided the impetus for one study which investigated the level of helping skills functioning of degreed alcoholism helpers who had no history of alcoholism and recovering alcoholic helpers who had no formal training beyond the high school level (Valle, 1977). The results of this and subsequent studies found there was no overall difference between recovering and degreed alcoholism helpers in terms of their functioning in helping skills. Rather than one group being more effective than the other, there was actually no difference. A further analysis of this particular study and those subsequent found that while there was no overall difference between the two groups, there were extreme scores within both groups. That is, some recovering helpers were found to be functioning effectively, but most were found to be performing at a very low level. There were also individual degreed helpers who were functioning effectively, although most were functioning at a low level. In both groups, the effectiveness of individual helpers was canceled out when the scores were grouped. Thus, there were high functioning helpers as well as low functioning helpers from each group. The issue is not whether one is a recovering alcoholic or if one has a degree, but rather at what level of skills is one functioning and what are the variables that account for some helpers being more effective than others.

TRAINING — THE KEY VARIABLE

Although a great deal of knowledge is yet to be found to adequately answer the question of who can be an effective alcoholism counselor, it is clear that much is already known. For example, the literature in the helping professions has concluded that what accounts in part for effective helping can be attributed to certain traits or skills of the helper. We also know that paraprofessionals can learn to function at levels commensurate with or, in some cases, higher than credentialed professionals and that traditional professional training programs may be for better or for worse. There also is evidence that no significant difference exists between the nonalcoholic degreed counselor and the recovering counselor who does not have a degree in terms of their overall level of functioning in helping skills.

A common theme found in the literature and which apparently accounts for a major portion of the difference is the variable of training. In a review of eighty-five articles on the effectiveness of paraprofessionals, Hoffman (1976) found that paraprofessionals can learn to function at highly effective levels of helping skills in twenty to forty hours of training. Valle and Anthony (1977) found that both recovering alcoholism helpers and degreed alcoholism helpers can learn to function at effective levels of helping skills in a thirty-hour training program if the training was systematically taught and primarily skills-oriented in content. Training alcoholism helpers in general knowledge and *about* helping skills was found to be inferior to training specifically *how to* function at effective levels of helping skills. This leads one to the conclusion that the issue of who can be an effective alcoholism helper cannot be separated from the issue of training. Both recovering alcoholics and professionally trained helpers have strengths and assets to bring to the alcoholism field. Both also have their deficits. Training is the one variable that can help those desiring to be alcoholism counselors to identify their strengths and improve upon their skills while also learning to deal with their limitations. A trademark of a profession is the degree to which quality training is made accessible to potential helpers.

Chapter 4

A HELPING MODEL FOR
ALCOHOLISM COUNSELORS

ALCOHOLISM counselors represent a diversified group of helpers who draw upon a variety of helping and therapeutic strategies in their role as counselors. In the absence of a specific helping model relevant to alcoholism, counselors have had to settle for a smorgasbord of techniques, modalities, and theoretical orientations. An abundance of conferences, workshops, seminars, and schools have emerged to provide alcoholism counselors with the opportunity to develop their helping skills. These efforts, however, have tended to emphasize increasing one's knowledge *about* helping alternatives rather than teaching counselors *how to* systematically be more effective in their helping roles (Valle & Anthony, 1977).

The lack of a systematic helping model for alcoholism counselors lowers a counselor's potential for having a constructive impact on clients. When counselors have a vague conception of goals and the process by which they will achieve these goals, helping becomes a haphazard and hit-or-miss process with the probability of success left to chance. If alcoholism counseling is to make its mark as a profession, it is imperative for counselors to have a clear understanding of what it is they strive to accomplish in a helping encounter and the procedure by which this will be achieved. Dabbling in the latest helping technique without a conception of its relation to the entire helping process has a confusing and fragmenting effect on helpees. When the alcoholic person comes for help, he or she has experienced enough disorder and chaos and needs more than a floundering helper!

One of the most thoroughly researched and applied helping models for counseling and psychotherapy has been developed by Carkhuff (Carkhuff and Berenson, 1977). The Carkhuff model has been successfully implemented in correctional settings (Carkhuff, 1974), mental health settings (Anthony, 1978; Carkhuff, 1969; Valle & Marinelli, 1975), university-based training programs (Anthony et al., 1977), educational settings (Berenson, 1971; Hefele, 1971), health care (Anthony & Carkhuff, 1976), and alcoholism (Valle, 1975, 1977). The Carkhuff model has been particularly useful in alcoholism counseling, as it has at its roots substantial research evidence which concludes that effective helping is a direct function of the helper's skills rather than educational background or formal credentials. Alcoholism counselors have demonstrated that when trained to function at an effective helping skills level, they can indeed function at levels equal to, or higher than, most professional helpers trained by traditional methods (Valle, 1977).

The impetus for the Carkhuff model is based upon an extensive body of evidence accumulated over the past two decades which concludes that helping and all human relationships may be "for better or for worse" (summarized in Carkhuff, 1969, and Carkhuff & Berenson, 1977). The constructive or destructive effects of our helping depend in part upon the level of interpersonal skills offered by helpers. Helpers who offer high levels of interpersonal skills help people, those who offer low levels harm people, and those who offer moderate levels of interpersonal skills do not make a difference. The interpersonal skills receiving the most research support are those involving the levels of empathic understanding, positive regard or respect, genuineness, and concreteness. The use of these interpersonal skills by helpers is guided by the phases of learning in which helpees engage in order to change constructively. These phases involve self-exploration, self-understanding, and action. Thus, the Carkhuff model can be understood in terms of what it is the helpee must do to change constructively and what it is the helper does to facilitate this change. These dimensions of the Carkhuff model will be described briefly in the following paragraphs.

HELPEE DIMENSIONS

The Carkhuff model describes the process by which clients

learn to change as involving self-exploration, self-understanding, and action. The helpee dimensions of exploring, understanding, and acting are intimately related to the helper dimensions of empathy, respect, genuineness, and concreteness. In fact, as the client explores, understands, and acts, his/her repertoire of responses is increased and thus the ability to act effectively. Helping in this model is a process of growth by which helpees change into helpers.

The model is particularly compatible with alcoholism counseling which has its roots embedded in the concept of one alcoholic helping another alcoholic. The dimension of exploration involves the helpee exploring where he or she is in relation to his/her world. It involves not only exploring where one thinks he is, but also where one really is. The high level of denial and low level of awareness about alcoholism require a thorough exploration process by alcoholic helpees. High levels of exploration enable the helpee to examine his relationship to alcohol, while serving as motivation to understand himself and his relationship to alcohol more thoroughly.

The understanding dimension involves the helpee building upon the base of exploration to the point where he understands himself and where he is in relation to where he wants or needs to be. Greater emphasis is placed upon gaining insight into oneself and one's behavior to the extent that responsibility for being alcoholic and for recovering is personally accepted. It is in this phase that major breakthroughs are made with alcoholics, as it is here that the alibi system breaks down and the person begins to own responsibility for drinking. Insight, however, does not of itself translate into action. The understanding phase then sets the stage for the final helpee dimensions of acting.

The emphasis in the action phase of learning is placed upon systematic programs that teach or show the helpee how to get where he or she wants or needs to be. It is not enough for a person to understand his problem with alcohol. He must learn how to take the steps necessary to remain free of alcohol and function effectively. This may require a variety of specific helping programs, depending upon the needs of each particular helpee. A common pitfall among alcoholism counselors is to gloss over the specifics of how one can maintain sobriety. It is not enough to just tell a person to abstain from alcohol. People need to be taught step-by-step how this goal can be attained in a manner that is progressive and constructive. The action phase stresses the importance of developing such systematic, step-by-step programs used to attain the goals identified during the understanding phase. The emphasis here is on teaching helpees how to systematically develop and implement relevant courses of action to get where they want or need to be.

Each of the helpee dimensions is measured by a 5 point scale which facilitates a counselor's application of the helper dimensions. Exploration, understanding, and action constitute the learning phases necessary for constructive change. Each phase is related to the other, making the process a continuing cycle of growth.

HELPER DIMENSIONS

The helper dimensions include the skills that effective helpers need to possess in order to involve helpees in exploring themselves, understanding themselves, and acting in ways that promote growth and constructive change, i.e. high levels of empathy, respect, genuineness, and concreteness. Five-point scales have been developed to assess these dimensions where level 3 is definded as the minimally effective level of functioning on each of the scales. While the scales themselves have many limitations, they have been used extensively in research and provide an important means by which helpers can measure their functioning on the core dimensions. Alcoholism counselors utilizing this model have the advantage of being able to constantly monitor their functioning. Accountability then is built into the model and can be referred to by individual counselors desiring to improve their level of functioning as well as by supervisors desiring to maintain high levels of counselor performance.

Empathy is the ability of the helper to respond to the feelings and reasons for the feelings of the helpee in such a manner as to communicate his/her understanding of the helpee. In empathic understanding, the emphasis is upon the helper's depth of understanding rather than his ability to "technique" it. This involves the helper's ability to merge his experience with the experience of the helpee and communicate this understanding to the helpee. The most potent form of empathic understanding is communicated by the helper's manner rather than his/her mechanical response and tends to be a blend of depth reflection from the client-centered school and the moderate interpretation of the psychoanalytic school (Carkhuff & Berenson, 1977).

The dimension of helper respect for the helpee as a person of worth is best communicated through the vehicles of human warmth and understanding. Respect, however, is not always communicated in a warm, soft tone of voice. Respect may, at times, be communicated in anger or disappointment. The communication of respect serves to break the isolation of the helpee and helps establish a basis for empathy.

The dimension of genuineness involves the degree to which a helper is congruent and sincere in the helping relationship. It is important to recognize that genuineness can have a negative impact when it is employed in a manner that detracts from what is effective for the helpee. Thus, genuineness is not a free license for the helper to do or say whatever he/she wills in a helping relationship. While the helper is always working toward a fully sharing relationship, he must be guided by what is effective for the helpee.

Concreteness involves the specific and direct expression of feelings and experiences. It serves to ensure that the helper's responses stay on "target" and are accurate in terms of the helpee's feelings and experiences. Concreteness encourages the helpee to attend to specific problem areas and emotional conflicts while avoiding abstract and vague issues.

The helpee is guided through the phases of learning by the helper's level of helping skills that facilitate this learning. Helping skills incorporate the helper dimensions of empathy,

4 helper dimensions important in counseling

respect, genuineness, and concreteness and serve to help helpees explore themselves, understand themselves at deeper levels, and act in order to change. Helping skills involve both responsive dimensions, where the emphasis is on responding to the helpee, and initiative dimensions, where the emphasis is upon facilitating change based upon deeper levels of understanding. The helping skills incorporated in the responsive and initiative dimensions include attending, responding, personalizing, and initiating.

Attending skills involve the counselor's ability to demonstrate that attention is being given to the helpee as a unique person. They include those nonverbal behaviors and environmental variables that communicate attentiveness. Such things as eye contact, body posture, facial expression, personal appearance, and atmosphere communicate the helper's attending skills or lack thereof.

Responding skills involve the counselor's ability to communicate to the client an accurate understanding of what he/she is experiencing and feeling. In order to respond effectively to clients, counselors need to communicate that they understand what the client is feeling and the reasons for their feelings. Helpers initially need to respond to the feeling and content of the helpee's experience at an interchangeable level and gradually respond at additive levels. Responding interchangeably is usually a reflection of the helpee's feelings and reasons for the feelings, whereas responding additively goes beyond reflection. Additive responses communicate the helper's understanding by responding to what the helpee is feeling at a deeper level than what is being expressed. Going beyond what the helpee expresses involves the ability of the helper to personalize the experience for the helpee. Personalizing skills are demonstrated when the counselor identifies the role the helpee is playing in either helping or hindering recovery. A counselor who personalizes the experience for the helpee helps him to take responsibility for his actions by personalizing the meaning, personalizing the problem, personalizing the feeling, and personalizing the goal. By using these responsive skills, the helper is preparing the helpee to take the necessary action steps to change. The use of counselor initiative skills facilitates the helpee to act in ways whereby he may reach his goals.

Initiating skills include the counselor's ability to "operationalize" goals and to initiate steps, schedules, and reinforcements to achieve these goals. Operationalizing goals means defining goals in observable and measurable terms so that the helper can tell when the helpee has reached the goal. Initiating steps to the goal include the development of a first step and then intermediary steps to the goal. Initiating schedules means specifying the starting and the completion dates for each step so that the helper and helpee know not only what is to be done, but also when it is to be done. Initiating reinforcements involve the development of positive and negative reinforcements, so the helpee is encouraged to continue taking action until his or her goal is attained.

The helper skills of attending, responding, personalizing, and initiating include the dimensions of empathy, respect, genuineness, and concreteness. The relationship of these helping skills to the phases of learning that the helpee goes through is demonstrated in Figure 1.

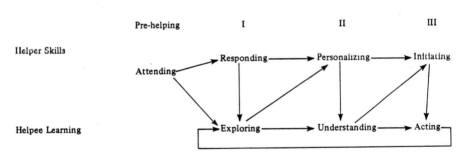

PHASES OF HELPING

Figure 1. (From BEYOND COUNSELING AND THERAPY, SECOND EDITION by Robert R. Carkhuff and Bernard G. Berenson. Copyright © 1967 by Holt, Rinehart and Winston, Inc.; Copyright © 1977 by Holt, Rinehart and Winston. Reprinted by permission of Holt, Rinehart and Winston.)

The Carkhuff model has been applied successfully in a variety of in-patient and out-patient alcoholism settings and has many strong points. Its emphasis upon functional skills rather than formal credentials has enabled alcoholism counselors to increase their level of effectiveness to levels that are equal to, and in some cases higher than, other professional helpers (Valle, 1977). Moreover, it is a model that enables counselors to assess their own progress as well as the progress of their helpees. It also provides a framework for counselors to conceptualize the helping process with considerable room for incorporation of other specific modalities within the overall model. For instance, a counselor may draw upon specific behavioral techniques during the action phase or rely upon insight modalities during the exploring and understanding phases. The important element is that within this model, counselors can help alcoholic people understand their illness and take action steps to change their behavior in a manner that is systematic and specific rather than haphazard and vague. For the alcoholism counselor who is committed and courageous enough to be held accountable, the model's built-in evaluation components challenge the counselor to never settle for mediocrity. The model directs counselors to be constantly involved in expanding their outer edges of personal growth and effectiveness. Counselors who are content with less do not belong among the ranks of the New Profession.

Chapter 5

CONSUMERISM IN COUNSELING

RECENT years have witnessed an emerging force that is having an impact throughout the human services system — the right of consumers to influence the service process which affects their lives. The consumer movement is a force that has influenced most areas of society, including counseling practices. More and more consumers of counseling services are asking questions relating to accountability as well as what they can expect to receive from their involvement with a counselor. What rights to I have as a consumer? How are my records and other information I share with my counselor protected from disclosure? What safeguards can I expect from unethical or fraudulent practices? What difference will counseling make? What qualifications must counselors possess in order to perform these services? Are there any guarantees? Because these and similar questions are being asked by consumers with increasing frequency, it is incumbent upon counselors to be prepared with accurate responses and also to understand that consumerism is not a threat, but rather a catalyst toward improvement and greater effectiveness.

What the implications of consumerism for the alcoholism counselor are and how the counselor can respond creatively to the needs of consumers is the primary focus of this chapter. It is this author's firm belief that the counselor should be the primary advocate for the consumer and that the counselor has a vital role to play in making consumerism a positive and integral part of the rehabilitation process. Alcoholism counselors, beyond all other helping professionals, have a unique opportunity to respond to consumer needs, since many have been consumers of alcoholism services themselves.

Consumerism in counseling refers to the parameters of the relationship between the party dispensing services and the recipient of those services (Sue, 1977). It is concerned with such issues as specifying clearly what the rights of clients are, identifying what it is that counselors do, why they are doing it, how it is done, and what outcomes can be expected. An implicit goal of consumerism in counseling is to have the consumer become an active participant in the process rather than a passive recipient. Counselors must realize that in addition to being accountable to bosses, supervisors, funding agencies, etc., they are accountable to their clients as well. Providers of alcoholism services can no longer afford the luxury of viewing themselves as a separate entity that can function independent of consumer needs. A mechanism for interdependence among providers (counselors) and consumers (clients) must be created if alcoholism counseling as a profession is to emerge from under the scrutiny of the consumer movement a viable helping resource for people with alcohol problems.

While the impact of the consumer movement is being felt throughout the human service network, perhaps no service is so close to the influence of consumers as are alcoholism services. Unlike most specialty areas which have been gradually forced to respond to consumer needs, alcoholism services have relied heavily upon consumers for their direction and delivery of services (Staub & Kent, 1973). Historically the self-help concept of one consumer helping another has carried the major share of services to alcoholic people. As a result of the persistent dedication of consumers, found in such movements as Alcoholics Anonymous and Al-Anon, services to alcoholic people are at an unprecedented level. The impact that consumers can have is dramatically felt in the alcoholism field as, even with increased federal and state funding for alcohol services, there is a high regard and emphasis placed upon the contribution one alcoholic can make to another's recovery.

Alcoholism counselors bear the primary responsibility for ensuring that clients' rights are protected. Counselors are also in a unique position to not only advocate consumer rights but also to influence the system in a manner that will make services more responsive to consumer needs. One way of accomplishing this is to develop an approach to counseling where the involvement of consumers in the rehabilitation process is encouraged.

It has been established that a relationship exists between consumer involvement in the rehabilitation process and the achievement of therapeutic goals (Thursz, 1969). That is, counselors who are responsive to consumer needs and actively involve them in the helping process are more likely to have better results. In one community program, a systematic model for involving consumers has been developed and successfully implemented that has served both to facilitate consumerism and enhance the quantity and quality of services to alcoholic people. This program will be briefly described as it represents a model for consumer involvement that is both therapeutic and practical.

CONSUMERISM IN ACTION: THE TAUNTON MODEL

Consumer involvement in the planning, delivery, and evaluation of community alcoholism services has been an essential component of the Taunton (Massachusetts) Alcoholism Counseling and Drop-In Center since its inception (Valle, 1975). This policy grew out of the Center's origin as a project funded by the Massachusetts Division of Alcoholism and sponsored by the Greater Taunton Council on Alcoholism. The Council is made up of members from local Alcoholics Anonymous and Al-Anon groups, citizens of local communities, and representatives of human services agencies.

The challenge of the Taunton Center was to develop a mechanism for processing over 300 service requests a week with a limited paid staff, a task which is being accomplished by actively involving consumers in the delivery of services. The operations of the Taunton Center include drop-in services, counseling, referral, advocacy, information, and education services.

The facility includes a drop-in lounge area which offers mutual group support to alcoholic persons and their families seven days a week from 9 AM to 9 PM. The support that consumers provide to one another is facilitated by a hot cup of coffee, comfortable surroundings, and people willing to listen to another person's problems. The lounge area is maintained by consumers who take responsibility for all aspects of its operations.

In the evening and on weekends the Center is staffed by "community staff," made up of consumers who have received services at the Taunton Center and volunteers who are interested in alcoholism. These persons, who are trained by the paid staff, operate the drop-in service without direct supervision and often provide clients with services which would be furnished by professional staff during normal working hours.

Several forms of counseling are available at the Center, some provided by the paid staff and others by consumers. These alternatives include therapy groups for alcoholic people, individual counseling, group therapy for spouses of alcoholic persons, couples' groups, discussion groups, and groups for children of alcoholic parents.

Although counseling and therapy are considered primarily the responsibility of the professional staff, it has been the position of the Center that professionals do not have a corner on the helping market and that consumers can also be valuable therapeutic aides. This view is confirmed by both the literature (Carkhuff, 1969; Truax & Lister, 1970) and the experience of the Taunton Center. How valuable consumers become as therapeutic aides depends on the provider's skills in selection, training, and supervision of consumers who serve in this capacity.

Since clients often need to make use of existing resources, referral is a critical program component at the Center. Consumers who staff the Center are provided with a guide to existing services in the area, along with instructions on how to complete a referral. Often consumers are involved in transporting clients to the referral sources, in following up clients who return to the Center, and/or as advocates for the alcoholic person in contacts with resources that may be resistant to helping the patient. Consumers who demonstrate skills and who are trained by the professional staff can also perform advocacy functions through involvement in training programs, by consulting with other agencies concerning clients with alcohol-related problems, and in educational activities, particularly as speakers representing the Center before community groups, schools, and the general public. When a consumer and a professional appear together as a team to speak at a community function, the impact is profound.

To assure that providers and consumers will wholeheartedly support consumer involvement in the delivery of services, it is essential to have a systematic progression of involvement clearly defined. Four fundamental principles for motivating consumers must be put into effect by providers if the consumers are to maintain enthusiasm and reap genuine benefits from the process. These principles are as follows:

1. The client must be involved in formulating his own rehabilitation plans.
2. Providers need to focus on the assets of the consumer.
3. For each step of the process, significant rewards must be available for the consumer.
4. Consumer involvement is meaningless unless consumers know that they can have an impact on the system; therefore, there must be a mechanism which gives consumers power.

SYSTEMATIC PROGRAM FOR CONSUMER INVOLVEMENT

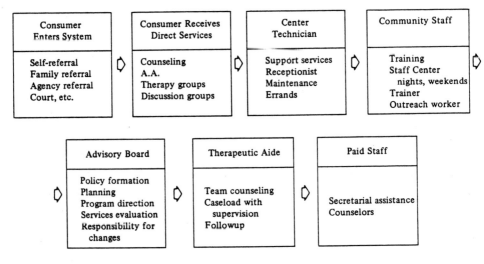

Figure 2.

Figure 2 represents a schematic presentation of the process for involving consumers at the Taunton Center. Unless the new client's particular situation warrants immediate referral to other service systems, he or she is offered direct services by the Center. These services provide the vehicle for involving clients gradually in helping others with similar problems. For example, when consumers use the drop-in lounge in the evening, they become aware that consumers like themselves are staffing the center. Their growing awareness that they themselves can be significant agents in serving others may be a crucial factor in rebuilding their damaged self-concepts, a condition prevalent among those affected by alcoholism. The consumer can then become a technician offering his or her services, whether for maintenance, reception, or managing duties, as an integral part of the total program.

When a consumer-technician is ready, he or she can become a community staff member. At this level, consumers take on more responsibility for direct services, with training by the paid staff a vital aspect. Monthly training meetings are held to sharpen the skills of the community staff, to provide an opportunity for discussion of problem areas, and to acquaint new consumers with the program of the Center. Becoming a community staff member requires a higher form of commitment from the consumer, as at this level he may be assigned to assist new consumer trainees in learning skills. A community staff member might also act as an outreach worker, linking the services of the Center to his neighborhood or representing the Center at speaking engagements in the community.

The next step involves increasing the responsibility and commitment of consumers by giving membership in the advisory board of the Center to those who choose to join it. This board, elected by and entirely composed of consumers, meets biweekly to plan, evaluate, and implement changes in the Center's program. Through this body, consumers are able to exercise power as they become a part of the decision-making process themselves. This board meets with the director of the Center, selects its own consumer representatives to serve on the Center board, and becomes involved in all aspects of operating the Center, from minor decisions to very difficult ones. This provides the consumer with an appreciation for the complexities involved in managing a human service agency and also provides an excellent training experience to prepare consumers for potential entry into the alcoholism field as providers.

As consumers progress through these stages of involvement, their unique skill and potential for helping become evident. The challenge to providers is to tap these resources and channel them in a manner which improves the overall delivery of services. This is accomplished at the Taunton Center by utilizing consumers as therapeutic aides. At this stage, consumers may become members of a counseling team, become counselors with separate caseloads under the supervision of a professional, and participate in follow-up services.

While the Taunton model represents a systematic progression of consumer involvement, no judgment is made as to the value of one stage over another. Although it is desirable for clients to progress through each step, the contribution made by consumers at stage three (Center technician), for example, may be as valuable to the individual as the contributions made by one who has reached stage six (therapeutic aide). The most important objective in consumer involvement is to accurately match the particular level of contribution the consumer is capable of making with the appropriate stage of involvement. Whatever the course of action pursued, it must be in the best interest of the consumer.

The involvement of consumers, working in cooperation with paid staff, in the actual planning and delivery of services has created a flexible program with built-in accountability to consumers. Bringing together the depth of experience of consumers and the expertise of professionals provides a program with a unique combination of resources and increases the potential for meeting diverse client needs. Counselors can facilitate the involvement of consumers by first understanding their needs and then creatively designing ways for those needs to be met. The Taunton Model is one example of how consumerism can be an asset to both the consumer and the provider.

GUIDELINES FOR COUNSELORS

In addition to taking an active role in involving consumers in the actual planning, delivery, and evaluation of alcoholism services as is suggested above, there are some specific steps counselors can take to demonstrate their responsiveness to consumers.

If consumers are to make responsible decisions, they must have accurate information to aid them in their choices. The best source for this information is the counselor who should be able to articulate clearly what alcoholism counseling is, how it is accomplished, and what can be expected from it. It is up to the counselor to clarify any confusion that may exist and to honestly label the services that are performed. Counselors should encourage clients to ask questions about the procedures involved in counseling, the fee structure, and the general operational procedures. To facilitate this, counselors can prepare a written handout that describes what counseling is, what qualifications a counselor must possess, the approach that is likely to be used, what the fee structure is, and how the client can influence the process through participation and feedback. During the initial interview, it is wise to have a short discussion about the counseling process to set the stage for open communication between the counselor and client. This also provides a good opportunity for clients to ask any questions they may have. One of the more prevalent reasons for impasse in counseling (the sense that you've gone so far in counseling and can't seem to get any further) is a result of leaving aspects of the counseling process vague. If such issues are not clarified in the beginning, it is likely that future therapeutic gain will be impaired.

Alcoholism counseling can be conducted in a number of different ways; however, counselors should be able to offer a brief description for the consumer to enable him or her to decide whether to use the services. Such a description should be written and should cover the following points:

1. A brief definition of counseling.

2. A statement of the counselor's qualifications — what training and experience the counselor has.
3. A description of the counseling process — how it happens, what approaches may be used, etc.
4. An explanation of operational procedures — when each session begins and ends, how many sessions are involved, what the fees and procedures for payment are, etc.
5. An explanation of how the consumer and counselor will evaluate what has occurred in counseling.
6. A statement specifying mutual responsibility for what transpires during counseling and for its results.
7. A statement encouraging the clients to ask any questions or discuss any concerns they may have.

SOME CONCERNS ABOUT CONSUMERISM

Consumerism is a concept that is held in high esteem in our society, yet when consumerism in counseling is advocated, certain problems and concerns arise. Involving consumers in the helping process described in the Taunton Model Program does have its problems. For example, the transition from consumer to provider often creates role conflicts that can threaten one's sobriety if considerable interpersonal conflicts are experienced for which the consumer is unprepared. Consumers who become providers may have unresolved personal issues which need to be attended to. If these issues are ignored, the consumer-turned-provider may be prone to utilize his or her job to keep sober or to work out personal conflicts. This invariably affects job performance and can defeat the very purpose of involving consumers in delivering services. In addition, the experience of the Taunton program reveals three problem areas that are likely to arise when implementing a consumer-oriented service:

1. The problem of overzealous helper: A consumer acting as a helper may unconsciously seek to fulfill his/her own needs at the expense of others. It is not uncommon to be confronted with overzealous helpers who, in their attempt to give service, actually inflict harm. Therefore, it is crucial for counselors to be aware of consumer needs and to

direct the energies of consumers into constructive channels.

2. Failure of consumers: It is not uncommon to be faced with the problem of consumers overextending themselves in trying to help and, consequently, facing failure. The counselor needs to be consistently sensitive to this possibility, or serious setbacks for the consumer may result. Such overextensions should be prevented through training and supervision. If this is not possible, and a consumer becomes a detriment to the program, it may be necessary to terminate his/her activities. When this happens, it is important for the counselor to handle the termination in such a manner that the consumer views his or her entire relationship with the program as a significant growth experience.

3. Professional resistance: A professional may resist consumer participation for several reasons. Some professionals are unable to deal with the threat of others less trained than themselves providing services, or they may tend to undervalue the importance of a consumer's contribution. Invariably, such undervaluing is evident to the consumer. From another perspective, the professional who is too eager to involve consumers may also be biased to the extent that he or she is blind to the faults of particular consumers.

There are other concerns that arise which relate to the broader implications of consumerism in counseling. This chapter has focused primarily on the rights of consumers; however, counselors need to recognize that consumers also have responsibilities, and perhaps as much attention needs to be given to identifying responsibilities as is given to consumer rights. Some issues counselors need to struggle with are the limits of consumerism and how far consumerism should go. Taken to its ultimate conclusions, consumerism could mean greater external regulation of counseling unless alcoholism counseling as a profession resolves these issues for itself. Could we actually defeat the purpose of consumerism by providing too much information which only serves to confuse the public?

Such dilemmas need to be considered, and resolutions must be provided by those who are in the field.

Consumerism in alcoholism counseling is a concept whose time has come. Counselors who want to remain at the cutting edge of their profession will struggle with the problems inherent in creatively responding to consumer needs. To do so is to grow as a profession and as helpers. To avoid the issue is to stagnate. For alcoholism counselors, there is no alternative.

Section II

ISSUES FOR THE PRACTITIONER

INTRODUCTION

$\mathbf{A}$ PROFESSIONAL counselor must possess an understanding of his/her role, obligations, and responsibilities in order to function effectively. In this section, some of the prevalent issues which may influence his/her effectiveness will be discussed.

The first issue to be dealt with is burn-out. Chapter 6 explains the concept of burn-out and suggests ways for counselors to minimize its negative impact. Chapter 7 discusses the importance of ethics and values in counseling. Examples of unethical practices are given, as well as perspectives for establishing a relevant code of ethics. The eighth chapter focuses on some common obstacles that hinder counselor performance, including elements derived from counselor and client perspectives. Chapter 9 stresses the importance of supervision for counselors. A supervision model for alcoholism counseling is suggested, and a description of some of the contemporary methods used in supervision is provided. The last chapter, Chapter 10, deals with three issues that profoundly affect the process and outcome of alcoholism counseling. Confrontation as a concept and as a technique is described from the perspectives provided by recent research. Understanding reluctant and resistant clients, as well as approaches that can be used in dealing with these clients, is another focus of this chapter. The final issue covered is termination. The importance of understanding the termination process is discussed, and suggestions are made for effective termination procedures.

Chapter 6

BURN-OUT: AN OCCUPATIONAL HAZARD FOR COUNSELORS

"As I look back on it now, I can only describe the feeling as one of being in a dark, bottomless pit. Everything was closing in on me; there seemed to be no way out. I had become immobilized by unknown fears and a sense of impending doom. As my shame and guilt mounted, my depression grew deeper. I withdrew more and more each day until the sense of isolation, a deep and desperate loneliness, had completely engulfed me. Afraid and unable to tell anyone of my problem, I began "covering up," even to the point of believing my own excuses and rationalizations. My paranoia only increased when friends began noticing and making helpful suggestions. I resented their interference! I had lost all sense of identity; my life had no direction, only insurmountable odds at every turn. I dreaded opening my eyes every morning because I knew it was only going to start all over again. Something which at one time had added to my life, given me pleasure, now had turned on me and was swallowing me up. I was no good; I was useless; I was burned out!"*

IT is a sad but common fact that many alcoholism counselors can personally identify with the feelings and behaviors shared by the counselor in the above account. In my experience as a counselor, supervisor, and trainer, I have come to believe that the burn-out phenomenon is the most frequently occurring and potentially dangerous hazard that a counselor will encounter in the course of his/her professional career. It is so common that it is almost predictable, yet little attention is given to the burn-out phenomenon by educators, trainers, supervisors, or program administrators. A great deal of attention is given to understanding the illness of alcoholism, the process

---

*A counselor's personal account of burn-out. My deep appreciation to Penny Hough for sharing this experience with others.

and skills of counseling, treatment planning, etc., but very little energy is expended in preparing counselors for the repeated, intense, and highly emotional encounters that are involved in a high human contact profession such as counseling.

For alcoholism counselors, the risks and potential dangers of burn-out are intensified by the very nature of alcoholism, the state of the profession in which alcoholism counselors practice, and the fact that many counselors have been personally close to the physical, emotional, and spiritual suffering caused by alcoholism. For the recovering alcoholic who works as a counselor, the necessity of understanding burn-out becomes crucial because one's vulnerability to relapse is highly increased. Burn-out is a tragedy to which all helping professionals are vulnerable; however, for the recovering counselor the vulnerability is intensified because it can be potentially life threatening as well.

In a field such as alcoholism counseling, the burn-out experience is more evident and its impact more profound due to the nature of the profession itself. For most human service professions, an identified body of knowledge exists which provides the practitioner with a framework for his/her role and guidelines by which to perform his role. The lack of a unified conception of what the role of an alcoholism counselor is and how one is to function in that role contributes to role confusion, indeterminate professional identity, and constant ambiguity, which serve to make one especially susceptible to burn-out. The absence of a unified formal training process contributes to a sense of unpreparedness that can surface under the stress of the job and thus feed a burn-out experience. Moreover, when burn-out does occur, there is no established support system from which one can expect help, a system that is provided by many other professions. The net result is that alcoholism counselors are particularly vulnerable. Therefore, this group needs to be prepared to recognize the symptoms of burn-out, to know how to cope with it when it occurs, and to know what can be done to minimize its impact.

WHAT IS BURN-OUT?

Burn-out is a term used to describe a condition with a series of common symptoms experienced by people in high human contact professions. While our focus here is to relate burn-out to alcoholism counseling, recent research has determined that burn-out is experienced by policemen, welfare workers, prison guards, psychologists, doctors, psychiatrists, counselors, nurses, clergymen, and other members of high stress, high human contact occupations (Maslach, 1976). When a person burns out or is in the process of burning out, one's emotional center breaks down. The counselor loses his empathy and the sense of caring about his clients, the job, and eventually his sense of self. Negative thinking begins to dominate the person's mind. Enthusiasm and anticipation wane and become replaced with pessimism, sarcasm, and, in some situations, hostility. Clients become a burden, small details become overwhelming, and avoidance behavior become the norm. One's energy level gradually decreases so that fatigue is frequent, and one experiences a sense of powerlessness over life events. In addition, a painful erosion of the person's confidence is felt so that he or she fears and then resents any added responsibility that normally would be considered routine. It is common for counselors who are in the process of burning out to experience psychophysiological symptoms of prolonged stress, such as tension headaches, insomnia, gastrointestinal disorders, anxiety, and depression. Frequently if the stress from burn-out cannot be alleviated on the job, it often surfaces in one's personal life. Sometimes the counselor is unaware of what is happening and wrongly attributes domestic conflicts to something that has gone wrong at home. The actual danger arising from this thinking pattern is that the counselor may inadvertently destroy the very source of support that he/she needs at a time when it is needed the most. When one's personal resources for coping become threatened, the impact of burn-out is even more profound.

While experiencing the effects of burn-out personally, the alcoholism counselor will affect his/her clients. They tend to become just "cases." As a counselor begins to burn out, there is a tendency to relate to clients or patients in a dehumanizing manner. Whereas normally counselors would treat clients with respect and understanding, burned-out counselors tend to respond with impatience and callousness. A counselor's response such as "You got yourself into the problem, now you'll have to get yourself out of it" is clear evidence that a counselor is burned out. He can no longer tolerate another's pain and finds his own resources for coping threatened. It is symptomatic for burn-out when a counselor admits to leading therapy groups for what he or she can get out of them. When a helper becomes aware of lapsing into the role of helpee in the helping relationship, it is an indication of a void that may be the result of burn-out.

When counselors experience burn-out, there is also a powerful effect on his/her colleagues. A burned-out counselor who goes unnoticed can deteriorate staff relationships and can have a disruptive influence on team functioning. If left untreated, the cynical, apathetic, and negative attitude of a burned-out counselor can permeate an entire staff. In a field as emotionally intense as alcoholism counseling, supportive interpersonal relationships among co-workers are imperative for survival. Great care needs to be taken to ensure that a counselor, in the midst of burning out, is attended to before the effects of burn-out destroy the bond so necessary for effective staff functioning in alcoholism services.

WHAT CAUSES BURN-OUT?

It has already been mentioned that the nature of alcoholism counseling itself, with its setbacks, low "success" rates, and emotionally draining effects, along with the status of the profession itself, is a highly contributing factor to burn-out. Inadequate training and a personal closeness to the effects of alcoholism were also mentioned as contributing to the vulnerability of alcoholism counselors to burn-out. Through my own experience with aspects of burn-out and through my observation of friends and colleagues who have experienced its effects in various degrees, I have identified several factors which emerge as contributing causes to burn-out. The factors identified have a common theme in that they appear to be based on certain myths and assumptions about alcoholism counseling as perceived by counselors.

Myth No. 1

A counselor should be "together" all the time and therefore should not experience problems like other people.

While one may regard Myth No. 1 as somewhat of an unrealistic attitude and therefore not that prevalent, it is surprising how many counselors subscribe to such an attitude unconsciously and sometimes even consciously. A common element among people experiencing the symptoms of burn-out is a gnawing sense of guilt over their own problems. When these counselors start recognizing potential trouble in their own lives, there is a recurring tendency to deny and repress problems. Being continually on the giving end seems to dull a person's awareness of one's own needs to express to others one's doubts, anger, fear, and conflicts. The end result is a very lonely and burdened individual. Ironically, while encouraging others to deal with their hurts daily, counselors sometimes deny themselves the right to say, "I'm hurting now and I need you." Being able to disclose their emotional needs to friends, colleagues, or loved ones is essential for counselors to maintain their emotional equilibrium. Failure to do so makes them particularly vulnerable to burn-out.

Myth No. 2

Helping another alcoholic to attain sobriety is all-fulfilling and of itself sufficiently rewarding.

One of the most prevalent experiences encountered by new alcoholism counselors is a jolting disillusionment with themselves and the work. After the initial excitement and the idealism associated with being a counselor diminishes, one is faced with certain realities. The realities of clients' low motivation to change, the absence of positive feedback, encounters with one's helplessness against a complicated and seemingly callous bureaucracy, minimal recognition, low wages, and limited success can slowly undermine one's attitude toward oneself and one's profession. The counselor finds that the satisfaction of helping is not enough. When this begins to happen, there is the danger that the counselor can become cynical and negative about clients, staff, and, worst of all, himself. Before accepting a position, it is important for a counselor to examine the assumptions which he or she may have about the kind of rewards and satisfactions expected from the profession. Many counselors who experience burn-out seem to have an unrealistic perception of what it is like to be a counselor and what they expect to receive from it.

Myth No. 3

Counselors' efforts will always be appreciated by clients.

Generally our society places a value on helping others. However, in the day-to-day experiences of counseling there is little expression of appreciation and gratitude, particularly from clients. The reality for many alcoholics is that they are resistant to treatment efforts and resent the very fact that someone is trying to "help" them. Most people troubled by alcohol initially fight the acceptance of their condition and, from the outset, perceive the counselor as an adversary rather than as a helper. The majority of clients are likely to be ambivalent, resistant, and hostile to the counselor's efforts. While this can be expected when dealing with the emotions of an addicted person, the emotional impact upon a counselor is not lessened. The very nature of alcoholism requires that counselors enter into the profession with the realization that what they do is often not appreciated by the people to whom they deliver services. Counselors must come to terms with their own needs to be appreciated and develop ways to fulfill these needs adequately in other ways. To expect appreciation from clients is to operate in a fantasy world which is likely to set the stage for disappointment and potential burn-out.

Myth No. 4

Having experienced alcoholism and gone through the recovery process is enough to be a good counselor.

While being recovered can provide a unique and valuable dimension to the helping process, counselors who rely on this dimension to the helping process, counselors who rely on this as the basis for their effectiveness soon realize that it is not enough. Counseling is a complex process that requires much more than support and understanding. When counselors realize this, they often are confronted with their own inadequacy, which in turn affects their performance. While being recovered can be a powerfully facilitative element in counseling another alcoholic, it can also be a stumbling block to effective therapeutic change. This is particularly evident when counselors generalize too much from their own experiences to the extent where the unique needs and experiences of clients are glossed over. While there are common elements in alcoholics, each person is unique and needs to be viewed with such a perspective. One alcoholic's answer for sobriety may not work for someone else. It is important for counselors to examine their own needs and to be careful not to assume that their own experiences will necessarily be applicable to others.

Myth No. 5

There is status and prestige in being an alcoholism counselor.

When a counselor arrives at the work scene, it is not too long before he realizes that a counselor's role is not what it appears to be. One soon realizes that status within the organization as well as financial rewards are inversely related to involvement in counseling. Generally it is not the counselor who gets community visibility or recognition. Rather he/she is stuck with "minding the store" so that other staff persons can go to meetings, speaking engagements, etc. The counselor soon realizes that other staff members receive recognition and stimulation and obtain a level of status within and outside of the alcoholism community, while he is the last to know of issues and the last to be invited to represent the agency. It is not too long before counselors also realize that in terms of financial rewards, they are low man on the totem pole. While counseling is the foundation for helping the alcoholic, it generally is given least priority in terms of funding and recognition. These factors contribute to a counselor's professional isolation and psychological distance, a sure setup for burn-out.

Myth No. 6

The counselor will be able to devote 100 percent of his/her efforts to helping clients.

One would naturally assume that being a counselor would involve mostly counseling, but in reality alcoholism counselors soon find there are many demands placed upon them, many of which conflict with the counseling of clients. Counselors sense their client's needs and attempt to meet them, but more often they are blocked in their helping efforts by institutional or agency policies. Many times a counselor's choices are limited by the needs of his/her colleagues or of the agency which at times conflict with clients' needs. Staff meetings, record keeping, bureaucratic necessities such as scheduling, forms, documentation, the push to terminate and close out cases, and the emphasis on statistics — all impinge upon the counselor's goal of providing undivided attention to one's clients. The reality is that most counselors spend less time counseling than they do coordinating activities and justifying bureaucratic demands.

WHAT TO DO WHEN BURN-OUT HITS

Burn-out can be experienced in varying degrees of intensity. The way in which burn-out is handled can make the difference between a temporary setback and a permanently damaged career. Below are listed some suggestions for dealing with burn-out that have emerged from the personal reports of counselors who have gone through the experience.

Recognize the Symptoms of Burn-out

Many counselors have said, "If only I had known what it was I was going through, maybe I would still be a counselor."

Unfortunately, the symptoms of burn-out often go unrecognized with tragic results to the individual and to the profession. When a counselor is aware of the symptoms, the likelihood of minimizing its impact is increased, and corrective steps can be taken before it is too late. Recognition of the symptoms of burn-out by other staff can also serve as a preventive measure.

Learn to Ask for Help

All counselors will be emotionally vulnerable at some point in their career as a result of the demands of their profession. Sometimes the most difficult step for a counselor is to ask for help, yet this is absolutely necessary if he or she is to maintain effectiveness. Staff members need to learn how to be helpers to one another as well as to receive help if they are to cope with the emotional burdens of their job. When you find yourself in need of help, ask for it.

Come to Grips with Your Limitations

Being blind to one's limitations can lead to false expectations and eventually to disappointment. Having an understanding of one's own limitations, the agency's, and those of one's colleagues helps to place things in perspective and avoids the myths and assumptions that can lead to burn-out. The role of clinical supervision is crucial to the process of coming to terms with one's limitations, because good supervision allows for the objective exploration of the counselor's strengths and weaknesses. A very common oversight in alcoholism services occurs when counselors, in their eagerness to be of help, overextend themselves. This can often result in failure, setbacks, and disappointments which can serve to erode a counselor's confidence. Every professional has limitations. Alcoholism counselors need to attend to this fact as much as they need to attend to other aspects of their work if burn-out is to be dealt with constructively.

Maintain Discipline and Structure, the Key Elements for "Holding on" During Burn-out

In the midst of the emotional turmoil caused by a burn-out experience, it is very easy to just drift and become passive in response to life events. When burn-out occurs, the sense of control over life is often jolted in such a way that an attitude of helplessness and despair sets in. Although this is a gradual and subconscious process, its effects are profound. When the symptoms of burn-out are recognized, it is important to practice strict discipline with respect to daily tasks and responsibilities, as there is a tendency to avoid responsibility, lose interest in daily activities, and become lethargic. To avoid translating these feelings into behavior, many have set up a strict schedule of activities to assure that they do not slip deeper into the burn-out syndrome. Some counselors have found it helpful to design daily goal sheets and activity lists as a means of measuring their accomplishments and also to serve as a self-reward system. In the midst of burn-out, minor accomplishments become significant and the importance of looking objectively at oneself is critical. Structuring one's schedule and disciplining oneself are valuable aids in dealing with burn-out.

Develop "Time-outs" On and Off the Job

Being constantly exposed to emotionally charged situations along with the pressure to be responsive and giving can gradually drain a counselor's resources. When a counselor senses that he is burning out, it is imperative that he distance himself from emotional encounters. This is often difficult for a counselor to do, but it becomes essential to survival. Counselors need to take time off when they feel their resources diminishing, even if it is just a day or two as a mental health break. Sometimes this may not be possible because of job demands, and for some overconscientious counselors, it may serve to create guilt. In such situations, a system of time-outs on the job can help one cope with burn-out. Time-outs are structured breaks during the day when the counselor distances himself from emotional encounters. This may be facilitated by having a short time of sharing with other staff members, a time when things are kept light and humorous. Carefully structuring the day to do paperwork or administrative chores for a period of time can serve as a relief from the intensity of counseling. Short walks out of the office or a time of brief exercise can do wonders for clearing the head from the burdens of clients. In one staff room, a dart board provided a healthy time-out release for staff when things began to pile up. If a counselor is creative in devising time-outs, he or she will find them invaluable therapeutic aids that can be crucial in sustaining equilibrium during a burn-out experience.

Diversify Your Responsibilities

Agencies that limit counselors to counseling become breeding grounds for burn-out. No one can be realistically expected to do counseling for forty hours a week and remain effective, spontaneous, and resourceful. Counseling is a demanding job that often is not appreciated by program administrators. Programs that require counselors to do only counseling tend to be vulnerable to inefficiency and low morale and thereby limit their effectiveness. This occurs most often in programs in which the director or administrator has had little or no experience in counseling. It is difficult to appreciate the intensity of counseling if one has never been involved in the process itself. While there are many excellent program directors who have never counseled, these persons are rare and usually careful in appreciating the needs of counselors for job diversification and good supervision. It would be a constructive step for agencies to replace part of a counselor's individual caseload with relevant activities in the community and to involve him or her in other aspects of the program. This not only provides a more effective use of staff skills, but also serves to reduce feelings of isolation and alienation experienced by counselors. Varying work responsibilities so that counselors are not constantly working directly with other people can serve to limit the effects of burn-out and prevent staff inefficiency.

CAN BURN-OUT BE PREVENTED?

Understanding what burn-out is, how it develops, and its effects leads us to consider whether or not burn-out can be prevented. Understanding and knowing how to deal with burn-out is as important as knowing the theories and techniques of effective alcoholism counseling. However, knowing how to respond after the fact provides little comfort to counselors and program administrators who want to prevent the hazards of burn-out.

After hundreds of hours of counseling and supervision counselors, I have come to the conclusion that burn-out in some form or degree is an inevitable reality for alcoholism counselors. In a field as emotionally intense as alcoholism counseling, the only type of counselor who is likely to escape an experience of burn-out is one who should not be counseling in the first place. Most alcoholism counselors are committed, conscientious, sensitive, and responsive people who are vulnerable to experiencing some form of burn-out at some time simply because they are caring people. Counselors who do not worry about burn-out have built such a wall of emotional defenses around themselves that they are likely to be distant, callous, or phony in their relationships with clients. For all other counselors, some form of burn-out is inevitable.

The issue is not whether the occurrence of burn-out can be prevented, as it is going to occur to most counselors to one degree or another. The real concern should be limiting its impact. The effects of burn-out do not have to be final if precautions and constructive action are taken when counselors first experience the symptoms. Unfortunately, our naivete about burn-out has often resulted in counselors leaving the field or experiencing lasting negative effects.

Listed and discussed in the following section are several steps that counselors and supervisors can take to help limit the negative impact of burn-out. Handled with skill and sensitivity, burn-out can in fact become a meaningful growth experience for the counselor, the staff, and the clients.

GUIDELINES FOR COUNSELORS
IN PREVENTING BURN-OUT

Be Informed About Your Position

Many counselors enter the field with minimal preparation and little formal training other than what has been gained through personal experience or volunteer work. The motivation for working in the field is never personally examined beyond the desire to want to help another alcoholic. While such motivation is commendable, it is naive to think that the personal gratification of helping another alcoholic is enough. Recovering alcoholics who are counselors must deal with the same pressures of daily living as any other professional. They will encounter the same bureaucratic obstacles, be driven by similar ambitions, and experience many of the conflicts other workers experience in the performance of their duties. It is important for alcoholism counselors to know such things as the salary range of the position, the opportunity for advancement, the supervisory expectations, the specifics of the job description, the caseload expected, the criteria used for evaluating performance, the paperwork involved, and the benefits before a position is accepted. One of the recurring themes reported by counselors who have burned out is disappointment and frustration with respect to their job. This can be traced to unrealistic expectations allowed to develop because the many details involved in a counseling position were never specified or understood.

Identify Your Goals and Evaluate a Position Accordingly Before You Say Yes

In order to avoid the bitterness that often comes with burn-out, it is important for counselors to have a good grasp of their personal goals. In talking with counselors who have burned out, many were unable to specify what their job expectations were. This often left them vulnerable to disenchantment. Counselors need to list their goals before entering the field and to only accept positions that measure up to a careful assessment of their potential for meeting those goals. Moreover, a goal-less counselor will experience limited success in helping his clients to be goal-oriented.

Maintain Your Own Growth at all Costs

Counselors who become involved in helping others often subtly neglect their own needs for growth. A counselor who has forgotten to attend to his or her own needs is a sure setup for burn-out. The impact of burn-out can be limited if counselors assure their own personal growth. This is often accomplished by developing open staff relationships, learning to express one's needs to supervisors, and by periodic training and educational opportunities.

Chapter 7

ETHICS AND VALUES IN COUNSELING

ALCOHOLISM counselors are continually gaining recognition from the public and other professionals as legitimate providers of helping services to alcoholics and their families. Counselor positions are not only sanctioned by the government but also are supported by a public that has bestowed its trust and confidence in the profession to provide quality services. One of the variables that contributes to public confidence is the assumption that those who perform the functions of a counselor are bound by certain ethical guidelines in the delivery of services. It has been mentioned earlier that one of the trademarks of an established profession is an accepted code of ethical behavior to which its members subscribe. While a code of ethics does provide broad guidelines of acceptable and unacceptable behavior, these guidelines are so general in nature that many of the ethical dilemmas counselors face in the course of practicing their profession are left up to the individual counselor to resolve.

The intent of this chapter is to explore some of the ethical issues involved in counseling, to provide a perspective for the profession in terms of establishing a relevant code of ethics, and to examine the place of values in counseling relationships. Counselors without a firm grasp of their own values and ethical orientations are likely to have a destructive impact on clients and the profession. It is up to the profession to provide direction to the individual practitioner as to acceptable ethical behavior and to discipline its members when ethical principles are violated. Ethical issues related to both the profession and individual counselors will be explored and their implications considered in the following paragraphs.

In the course of their functions, counselors are faced with ethical conflicts each day of which they may or may not be aware. Few professions have more potentially constructive or destructive effects on people than do the helping professions. The processes and outcomes are subtle, vague, disguised, and often invisible. While enjoying a relatively high degree of respectability, counseling and all therapeutic interventions have recently been questioned because of the uncertainty about what a therapist does, how he or she does it, and whether or not it is effective. An activity that is as widely practiced and that has such potential to influence for better or for worse as counseling has as much responsibility to pay particular attention to its ethical concerns as it does to its technical and methodological aspects. One result stemming from the proliferation of alcoholism services and the involvement of lay and professionally trained people in delivering these services is a myriad of approaches, techniques, and orientations used in helping the alcoholic. Unfortunately, alcoholism services have grown at such a rapid pace in recent years that little effort has gone into considering the ethical implications of such helping services and of those who provide them to the public. For example, many therapeutic approaches drawn upon by alcoholism counselors have little or no scientific validity with respect of their efficacy. Yet many counselors will attend a seminar or workshop on a therapeutic approach and begin applying the technique without considering the ethical implications of their newly acquired "skill" or without even considering whether or not they are qualified to begin practicing it. An avoidance of ethical considerations by counselors themselves and by the field in general can only have negative effects on the development of this profession toward full recognition and acceptance by the public.

ETHICAL NEUTRALITY?

For a period in the development of the counseling profession, considerable emphasis was placed upon the neutrality of counselors in terms of ethical and value issues (VanHoose & Kottler, 1977). This view contended that clients must be free from the influence of the counselor's values in order to completely determine their own. Being neutral was a way of demonstrating a counselor's respect for a client and the ability of the client to develop his or her own unique value system, as long as it was one that fostered health. While the motivation for the position of ethical neutrality is admirable, current thinking recognizes that "to continue a pretense of ethical neutrality is misleading and absurd" (VanHoose & Kottler, 1977). Every counselor has some notion of what kind of life would be best for the client and, by the very nature of the counselor's functions, takes positions that involve issues of ethics and values. The nature of helping itself reflects the value orientation that certain behaviors are good and certain behaviors are destructive. Counselors helping an alcoholic to abstain from drinking are reflective of values that regard continued drinking as being destructive to that person. Implicit in such a position is a notion of what is good or bad for a person or society. If we did not value a certain quality of life, there would be little, if any, therapeutic intervention in our society. Much of what counselors do cannot be separated from the context of human values from which they are operating. Whether implicitly or explicitly, counselors operate from an ethical and value system that influences behaviors, goals, strategies, orientations, and outcomes of clients (Ajzen, 1973). The counseling relationship involves an examination and confrontation of the client's values, the counselor's values, and how challenges to these values can be resolved in a healthful and growth-producing manner. To avoid issues of ethics and values in counseling is to ignore a vital part of one's humanity and a primary motivating force influencing one's behavior. Counselors cannot claim that they have no values nor that their values are of no concern to the client (Benjamin, 1974). The awareness of one's ethical and value orientation and the nature and scope of its influence on clients is a critical ingredient in effective counseling. Sensitivity, appreciation, and respect for the client's value system and the ability to constructively explore and examine its relationship to behavior are equally critical.

PERSPECTIVE ON ETHICAL STANDARDS

Ethics is concerned with how and why people make moral

decisions (Daubner & Daubner, 1970). Because ethics are based upon the ability of individuals to make choices, it is concerned with principles that ought to govern human conduct rather than those that actually do govern it (VanHoose & Kottler, 1977). The purpose of a professional ethical code is to provide some guidelines for "right" or "wrong" behavior. Professions which have ethical codes define for their members the basic principles that members in good standing ought to be following. Ethical codes help to clarify an individual's responsibility to clients and to society. They help to guide individual members of the profession in determining positions or standards when conflicts arise. For example, an ethical code for counselors helps to define the responsibilities of/client-counselor relationships, counselor-employer relationships, and counselor-society obligations as they relate to clinical practice. A code of ethics also serves to insure the protection of society from unscrupulous members and to insure the recognition and correction of individual behavior detrimental to the profession. An ethical code also serves to safeguard a professional's freedom and integrity (McGowan & Schmidt, 1962; VanHoose & Kottler, 1977).

While an ethical code does provide principles concerning a professional's responsibilities to clients, to society, and to the profession, it often does not solve individual problems that arise from clinical practice. For many helping professions, the code of ethics is often ambiguous, nonspecific, vague, and unenforceable. This tends to neutralize the effect an ethical code may have on individual behavior. Moreover, ethical codes serve to protect the professions as well as to protect the public from incompetent practitioners. VanHoose and Kottler (1977) identify three dangers that professions are protected from by ethical codes. One primary reason is to protect the profession from governmental interference; professions value autonomy and wish to avoid regulation by lawmakers. A second important reason is to promote harmony within the profession so as to avoid internal conflicts that can be divisive. For example, codes of ethics for therapists regard the criticizing of a professional colleague publicly or in the presence of clients to be unethical.

Thirdly, ethical standards protect the practitioner from the public by providing a defense against malpractice allegations.

When the development of ethical standards for alcoholism counselors is considered, several problems arise that make the task a difficult one. There are many views of what counseling is and what approach ought to be used in working with alcoholics. The specific roles and responsibilities of alcoholism counselors vary depending upon the setting, as do the training and educational backgrounds. These conditions lead to misunderstandings among other professionals, confusion within the profession, and uncertainty from the public of what can be expected of alcoholism counselors. There also is a problem in attempting to specify standards in a profession such as alcoholism counseling when there is competition for a counselor's loyalties. Counselors are often placed in situations where responsibilities to clients, employers, and the larger society are conflicting. Often such conflicts cannot be reconciled by standards and must be left to the individual counselor's own sense of which standards or values take priority. This process is often painful and risky for the counselor as he or she cannot always rely upon specific standards to bail him/her out of difficult situations. There will be situations where courage and risk-taking remain the only alternatives for the counselor.

PERSPECTIVE ON UNETHICAL BEHAVIOR

Although the majority of alcoholism counselors are competent, honest, ethical, and responsible individuals, there are those individuals who do behave unethically. This can be said of any profession. Such individuals may be operating out of ignorance of the ethical implications of their acts, or they may be consciously manipulating people and events to attain personal goals. In both circumstances, these individuals are dangerous to the welfare of their clients and pose a threat to the integrity and stability of the profession.

In order to have a perspective on unethical behavior, it is important to distinguish it from incompetent behavior. While incompetence is a part of unethical behavior, it is somewhat different. Incompetence refers to a lack of skill, ability, or qualifications to effectively perform certain functions (VanHoose & Kottler, 1977). The failure to recognize one's limits as a professional often results in the alcoholism counselor attempting to treat problem areas for which he or she has no specialized training. When counselors delve into areas in which they have not been trained when in fact they should refer the client to another professional, the counselor is demonstrating incompetence (Pietrofessa & Vriend, 1971). An unethical counselor is one who is unaware of the standards of the profession and yet proceeds to function as a counselor. Such an individual makes himself out to be a qualified professional when in fact he is not, as he has failed to acquaint himself with the ethical standards of the profession. An unethical counselor is also one who lacks the integrity to maintain standards of right and wrong as defined by the profession, the community, or the agency in which he or she works.

In considering some common examples of unethical behavior, it is important to keep in mind that counselors are human beings who make mistakes. When we speak of unethical behavior, we are talking about those actions or lack of actions on the part of the counselor, whether done through ignorance or by intent, that continue unchallenged or uncorrected. In the course of one's career as a professional, every counselor has at times behaved unethically. Counselors are human and errors are inevitable. When counselors do not investigate whether their actions are in line with ethical standards, when they choose to remain ignorant of the ethical implications of their behavior, or when they willfully violate accepted standards, they are being unethical. Counselors are not expected to be perfect human beings who always act ethically and responsibly, but individuals willing to refine techniques and, more often than not, act in an ethical and competent manner (VanHoose & Kottler, 1977).

Some examples of practices that can be considered unethical are discussed below. It is recognized that these may be mitigated by special circumstances where the determination of what is ethical or unethical is not clear-cut. The situations in the following discussion are provided to enable counselors to gain a perspective on unethical behavior and should not be viewed as standards in and of themselves. It is up to the profession to develop its own code of ethics and standards, and to see to their adherence. The following examples are taken from clinical practice and supervisory sessions with alcoholism counselors, and are presented as a vehicle for counselors to explore, examine, and determine their own perspective on ethical behavior.

Overinvolvement with Clients

Becoming personally involved with clients beyond appropriate limits as defined by the helper-helpee relationship is a common ethical conflict. Clients can become very attached to their counselor, enabling the counselor to take liberties not considered appropriate in a professional relationship. This may involve elements of emotional or physical attraction that can serve to avoid key therapeutic issues. It is not uncommon for clients to be grateful to the counselor for the effect they have had on their lives and to feel a strong emotional bond with their counselor. Issues of transference and counter-transference are common in therapeutic relationships and need to be understood and dealt with appropriately. Oversocializing with clients while a therapeutic relationship is being maintained can confuse clients and inhibit therapeutic gain. Clients represent various walks of life and often may be influential in the community. Using the therapeutic relationship as a means of obtaining favors, conveniences, or services is permitting the therapeutic relationship to be used as a vehicle for personal gain and is considered to be unethical.

Overidentification with Clients

Many alcoholism counselors are recovering alcoholics themselves and thus have an experiential dimension that can contribute significantly to helping other alcoholics understand their illness. However, making the assumption that one's own experience with alcoholism and the recovery process is similar to a client's experience is a sign of overidentification. Overidentification is disrespectful to the uniqueness of a client's experience and can be an obstacle to effective counseling. It is difficult to remain objective and to develop individualized treatment plans for clients when the counselor's view is distorted through overidentification. Appropriate self-disclosure can be an effective tool in counseling, but counselor disclosures shared to impress clients, to seek approval from clients, or to satisfy personal needs are examples of abusing the client-counselor relationship. What was good and effective for one person may not be good for another. To make such an assumption and to conduct a therapeutic relationship accordingly is unethical.

Encouraging Dependency in Clients

One of the primary goals in all therapeutic relationships is to enable clients to make decisions in their own lives and to take responsibility for their behavior. Counselors who continually give advice rather than help clients to explore alternatives and to arrive at their own decisions give clients the impression that they are not capable of making it on their own and that they need the counselor to function. Counselors who promote such dependencies, even if at the unconscious level, are behaving unethically. Seeing a client longer than is necessary is an example of counselor behavior that tends to produce dependence rather than independence. Counselors ought to be in touch with their own needs for approval, recognition, and power. Uncontrolled or unrecognized needs for approval can cause a counselor to refrain from confronting clients, to avoid setting limits and structure, and to fall into the trap of using the client-counselor relationship to fulfill personal needs. Attempting to rescue clients from the consequences of their behavior and allowing clients to feel that the counselor is solely responsible for the growth and positive change that occurs during therapy are indicators that the counselor is promoting a dependency.

Operating Beyond One's Competency

Alcohol problems rarely occur in a vacuum, which presents a dilemma for the alcoholism counselor. Most clients who have difficulty with alcohol experience disruption in some other aspect of living. In fact, it is unusual for a client to seek help for a drinking problem unless some other problem areas have initially emerged. It is more normative for one's job, family, or social life to become affected before it is recognized that alcohol is the primary reason for this disruption.

The dilemma facing alcoholism counselors is that often they find themselves confronted with problem areas for which they are not prepared or trained. When, for example, a client has a drinking problem but also is in crisis over a possible career change, experiencing psychological disturbance, and having problems with a marriage, the counselor must decide what is an appropriate course of action. Should the counselor attempt to deal with the client's drinking problem only and ignore the other problems? Should the client be referred to a vocational counselor to deal with career issues, a psychologist to deal with difficulties in coping psychologically, or to a marriage counselor for help with marriage problems? Which issue should be dealt with first? While the specific answers to these questions should be found through the vehicle of clinical supervision, it is clear that a counselor operating out of one's area of expertise is operating unethically. Counselors cannot afford the luxury of experimenting with their abilities when the welfare of a client is at stake. For other problems that alcoholics have, specialized resources are available and should be utilized. An effective counselor is aware of his/her own competencies, aware of referral resources, and prepared to make necessary referrals when he or she is not qualified to help. Attempting to treat problem areas beyond one's area of expertise is naive, dangerous, and unethical.

Confidentiality Issues

Confidentiality is a prevalent concern that clients have regarding their involvement in counseling or other helping activities. If a client does not feel confident that what is shared in a counseling relationship is confidential, he or she is likely to be reluctant to discuss sensitive matters. Confidentiality is an important counseling process issue as well as an ethical and legal one. Clients wonder what the counselor will do with the information that is presented in a session, what portion will become part of the record, what will happen to records, and how protective the counselor will be with this privileged information. Resistance in counseling relationships can often be traced to mistrust about how the counselor will regard confidential information. Counselors who permit confidentiality issues to be vague and unclear in a client's mind will always be limited in what they can accomplish with a client. It is not only a good counseling practice to inform clients about confidentiality issues at the very beginning of a therapeutic relationship, it is unethical not to do so. Counselors have an ethical responsibility to address themselves to the intricacies of confidentiality and to discuss with clients their expectations and concerns regarding confidential information.

Recent regulations which have specific implications for alcoholism counselors concerning the confidentiality of alcohol and drug abuse patient records have been developed by the Department of Health, Education and Welfare. According to these regulations, all programs and personnel of programs receiving federal or state funds or who have tax-exempt status are obligated to abide by these regulations. The regulations require treatment personnel to obtain written consent from the client for any information, whether recorded or not, before it can be released. Information that comes from another source, such as another treatment program, is also considered confidential. In addition to information about records, information about client presence or absence, attendance, or physical whereabouts and status is considered confidential and not to be released without written consent from the client (Mass. D.P.H., 1976). Exceptions to these regulations include situations where a client commits or threatens to commit a crime and cases of medical emergencies.

If clients commit or threaten to commit criminal acts, legal consultation should be immediately sought, as each state may have specific laws. Most states require counselors or therapists to notify public authorities and the person being threatened when such threats pose a potential danger to the health, life, or welfare of another person. When a client commits or threatens to commit a crime on the premises of the program or against personnel of the program, counselors are free to notify the necessary public authorities. However, if this is done, the suspect should not be identified as a client (Mass. D.P.H., 1976). Other exceptions include information given to researchers without the patient's consent as long as the report made by the researchers does not identify the patient. In addition, "no state and no agency or political subdivision of a state may require, for any reason, patient identifying information unless the receiving agency is legally required to hold information received in confidence. . . . In the case of any type of audit or evaluation to inspect the accuracy of records, the effectiveness of the program's administration, or its adherence to standards, information may not be requested or given unless the examiner furnishes a written statement that no record with patient identifying information will be made without notice to the program" (Mass. D.P.H., 1976). Also, qualified service organizations such as private labs or testing services are not required to obtain written consent, provided a written agreement with the program is made stating that the organization is bound by the same confidentiality regulations as the program. Agencies that are utilized for client referrals are not considered *qualified service organizations* if services are provided after the client has left the referring facility. In such situations, information can be given only if a written consent signed by the client has been obtained. If, however, one corporation operates several programs, communications between these program components would not require a consent form nor would communication between staff members within a program. In such situations, counselors may not be bound by law, but they are still subject to the maintenance of confidentiality as a matter of ethics.

In order for counselors to release information regarding a client, a written consent form must be signed by the client.

Such a form should be specific in nature and include the name of the program making a disclosure, the name of the person or organization receiving the information, the name of the client, the specific purpose of the disclosure, the nature and extent of the information to be disclosed, the date the consent is signed and when it expires, and the signature of the client. A global consent form is not considered sufficient. The regulations also define procedures for disclosing information to third-party payers, funding sources, lawyers, employers, criminal justice agencies, and families or friends.

Although the confidentiality regulations may be cumbersome and sometimes insensitive to treatment issues, they were designed with the goal of protecting the rights and welfare of clients. It is incumbent upon counselors to be thoroughly familiar with these regulations as they are legally and ethically responsible for upholding them. When questions regarding confidentiality arise that do not seem to be covered by current regulations, it is important for counselors to consult their supervisor and program attorney for advice. The risks to both the therapeutic relationship and to a counselor's career in making a poor judgment about confidentiality issues are too great for carelessness. Counselors who are viewed by their clients as protecting their rights and guarding privileged communication will foster trust and confidence in the therapeutic process.

The previously stated examples from clinical practice and supervision are some of the more common ethical issues with which alcoholism counselors must deal. Such a cursory review of examples of unethical behavior is intentional, as the profession must develop its own standards, design a means of monitoring and resolving ethical issues, and provide direction to the counselor regarding appropriate and inappropriate ethical behavior. To facilitate this process and the development of a more comprehensive format for examining ethical issues, suggestions are offered in the following sections.

Establishment of a Comprehensive Code of Ethical Standards for Alcoholism Counselors

It is essential that a comprehensive code of ethics be established to serve as a guide for determining appropriate and inappropriate counselor behavior. In order for this code to have direct counselor involvement, it would be most effective if developed and adopted by the professional association representing alcoholism counselors. An effective code should involve more than a few general statements of principles and should deal with all aspects of the counselor's role. A viable code of ethics should specify the standards expected of alcoholism counselors not only in their relationships with clients, but with the client's family, the client's employer, fellow counselors, colleagues in other professions, employer and supervisor, the community, and other human service agencies or programs. Ethical standards should also include guidelines regarding research and guidelines for maintaining levels of competency through continued education and training. In addition, a comprehensive code of ethics should deal with such matters as counselor competency, moral and legal standards, how one should present oneself to the public, and guidelines for appropriate professional conduct relating to all aspects of one's role. Each of the areas mentioned above should be regarded as a separate category requiring specific standards. The development of comprehensive ethical standards is a crucial step in the emergence of a profession. Such standards should come from within the profession rather than be imposed from without, reflect the actual role and functions of alcoholism counselors, and be continually reviewed and updated to assure their relevancy.

Establishment of a Committee on Professional Ethics and Conduct

In order for ethical standards to have meaning, there must be a mechanism for reviewing these standards, for developing new ones, for monitoring the conduct of counselors whose ethical practices are called into question, and for interpreting the standards for the field. A committee comprised of representative alcoholism providers should be established to provide information and to answer inquiries. Even the most comprehensive standards cannot deal with the intricacies and complexities encountered in daily practice and will need interpretation in regards to the application of the standards. The professional organization representing alcoholism counselors should develop such a committee and define its role for the field. In addition to monitoring, reviewing, and interpreting ethical standards, such a committee could be charged with determining procedures relating to registering complaints, evaluating information surrounding a complaint, and establishing disciplinary matters.

Development of a Casebook on Ethical Standards

A final recommendation involves the publication of a casebook on ethical standards to be widely circulated among alcoholism counselors, supervisors, and program administrators. Such a casebook could serve as a major reference that would include specific examples of ethical dilemmas frequently encountered in actual practice. It would draw from actual cases and could be designed in such a manner as to further clarify the standards that are developed.

With comprehensive ethical standards developed, a committee created to review, monitor, and interpret the standards, and a casebook of actual ethical problems encountered in practice published, alcoholism counseling will have made great strides towards its emergence as an autonomous, creative, and productive profession.

VALUES IN COUNSELING

The role of values in influencing and determining behavior is a complex topic beyond the scope of this work. There are, however, a few critical points that will be considered as they are crucial to counseling. There exists an extensive body of theory and research that deals with the role of values in human functioning (Raths et al., 1966; Rokeach, 1970; Scheibe, 1970; Simon et al., 1972). A consistent theme in this literature is that there exists an important relationship between values and behavior. It would follow then that counselors need to be thoroughly schooled in the understanding of values and how they affect behavior if they are to be effective in helping people change constructively.

As was mentioned previously, there was a time when a therapist was encouraged not to deal with values in counseling as it was thought that considering values would result in imposing one's values on the client and thereby inhibit the client's growth. It is generally recognized, however, that values are an integral part of human behavior and that therapists constantly encounter behaviors that cannot be worked through apart from dealing with a person's values (Kemp, 1967; Raths et al., 1966). The disposition of favoring one thing over another, of making choices or decisions, or of having preferences significantly influences the behavior of both the client and the counselor. Counselors need to become aware of their own values and understand how these influence their orientation to counseling theory and process, their behavior as a counselor, and the techniques or approaches they adopt. All major counseling strategies stem from a value structure that has a notion of the nature of man, society, and what constitutes constructive behavior. Counselors who simply adopt certain counseling techniques without being aware that they reflect a certain value structure are being naive and unethical. Counselors need to be aware of the underlying value assumptions behind their behavior and of how these assumptions influence their perception of the client and influence the goals, objectives, and preferred outcomes of the counseling process. In addition, counselors need to be aware of the value structure of their clients and of how they can help them explore their values. Helping clients clarify their own values, determine how their values affect their behavior, and examine the available alternatives helps to accomplish the goal of fostering individual responsibility for behavior.

Dealing with the effect values have on behavior raises several dilemmas for the counselor. Values of the client, counselor, and community may not often be in harmony. An important issue for the counselor is how he can help the client evaluate his values and the conflicts arising from divergent value systems without imposing his own values on the client. It is appropriate for counselors in the course of a meaningful counseling relationship to share their own preferences, attitudes, and values when such self-disclosure is helpful to the client. One must use great skill in presenting such material and recognize when it is appropriate for self-disclosure and when it is best to refrain from presenting one's own value orientation. When a significant therapeutic relationship is established and the client is able to use such information beneficially, counselors can have a great impact on client's self-exploration by disclosing their own values, as long as these are not imposed on the client. It should be viewed as one alternative among many that the client may choose. If such a sharing of values is used to facilitate client's self-exploration and understanding and used as a vehicle that enables clients to assume greater responsibility for their actions, then it can be highly therapeutic. In order for a counselor to carry this off effectively, one must be aware and secure in one's own values.

A person's values can also be used as a defense against taking risks and changing behavior. Just as values can help direct a person toward a goal, they can also serve to promote avoidance behavior. Counselors need to be aware of how values can be used constructively and destructively as motivators of behavior. Values serve to preserve one's self-image and therefore are capable of being used defensively to meet self-esteem needs (Hultman, 1976). For example, a person may regard the value of respect for authority as so important that he neglects to assert himself appropriately when he is being treated unfairly. In this case, the person is using values to escape a threatening situation. It may be more propagative and facilitative to point out how he or she is using those values as a defense against danger and then to teach him/her how to be assertive without being disrespectful. As Ellis (1973) has pointed out, many values are based upon irrational beliefs that serve to prevent the person from meeting his needs. When a person is using values as a defense, the purpose is to avoid or escape something feared or something that is threatening to his self-image. The fear of disapproval from others can cause a person to be overly compliant, polite, and accommodating, which in extremes can be self-defeating.

Counselors need to be aware that values are powerful motivators of both approach and avoidance behavior. Much of a client's resistance to change can be attributed to values that are used as defenses. These are often hard to detect, which is why they make excellent defenses. Effective counseling involves helping clients to consider the impact of values and beliefs for determining both constructive and destructive behavior.

Another value dilemma counselors may face in the course of their work is the conflict that arises when the practices or standards of the institution, program, or community one works for are contrary to one's own, or contrary to what may be helpful for a particular client. Societal standards are based upon the norm; however, counselors are often dealing with people whose behavior is not necessarily normative. Sometimes certain behaviors may be productive for the client but may be detrimental to those who will be affected by his or her behavior. There is no prescribed answers to such conflicts, but the counselor who is aware of his/her own values, the client's values, and the values of those who will be affected by a client's actions will be better able to process and resolve such issues in the course of counseling.

Helping clients to understand their own values and the relationship of these values to their needs, desires, and behavior is an essential part of the counseling process. By helping clients clarify their values, counselors may greatly enhance the client's ability to make decisions and to take responsibility for these decisions. To do so, counselors must be thoroughly familiar with their own values, understand how values relate to behavior, and be skilled in the process of helping clients explore these in the context of an open and unimposing relationship.

Chapter 8

OBSTACLES TO
EFFECTIVE COUNSELING

A COUNSELING relationship involves the dynamics of two or more individuals and therefore is influenced by what each contributes or fails to contribute to that relationship. The attitudes, values, beliefs, expectations, experiences, and commitments of both the counselor and the client affect the interpersonal process in a counseling relationship. Whether these factors have a contributing or inhibiting effect depends upon the counselor's awareness of such factors and his or her ability to deal with them constructively. This chapter will focus on some of the more common obstacles to counseling that alcoholism counselors have reported as being particularly frequent stumbling blocks. Because effective or ineffective counseling can be attributed to factors influencing both the counselor and the client, consideration from each perspective will be given to obstacles that tend to inhibit progress.

OBSTACLES FOR THE COUNSELOR

Role Confusion

One factor that inhibits progress in counseling is confusion regarding the role of an alcoholism counselor. Counselors are hired in detox centers, halfway houses, out-patient clinics, hospitals, courts, industries, and a variety of long-and short-term treatment facilities. While the tasks required in such programs call for counselors to provide counseling services, the actual duties of a counselor often vary depending upon the setting. A counselor's role in a detox center may be entirely different from the role of one working in a community outreach program. Counseling may have different meanings for different counselors, and the expectations of employers are often more defined by the goals of the particular program than by a consistent conception of what an alcoholism counselor actually does. Many counselors find themselves spending most of their time making referrals, writing notes, calling employers, meeting with families, or arranging for food, clothes, and housing rather than actually counseling. This often occurs in community programs where limited funds require a counselor to perform many of the duties usually delegated to other professionals. When a counselor spends most of his/her time coordinating rather than counseling, clients become confused as to what they can expect from a counselor. This can also create conflicts for the counselor, particularly if he expects to be involved in counseling but rarely has the opportunity to do so because coordinating activities takes up most of his time. In such cases, it is relevant to ask if the alcoholism helper is a counselor or a coordinator. If the role primarily calls for coordinating tasks, it may be more accurate to refer to the person as an alcoholism services coordinator rather than an alcoholism counselor. It has been established that client expectations have a great influence on the counseling process (Goldstein, 1971; Lazarus, 1974). Using titles that more accurately reflect the services to be performed helps minimize the creation of a false expectational set on the part of clients and serves to free counselors from the burden of trying to be all things to all people.

Role uncertainty is also evident when counselors are unsure as to whether they should be specialists or generalists. A counselor who views himself as a generalist often feels compelled to deal with all the conflicts an alcoholic may be having, whereas a counselor who regards himself as a specialist may limit his intervention solely to drinking issues. Should an alcoholism counselor deal only with the issue of drinking, or should he or she include in his/her services those problems that a client may have in addition to, or resulting from, alcohol abuse? Some counselors may do both; that is, with some clients they focus only on the drinking issue and with others they deal with related life problems as well. The danger inherent in this is that clients may become confused, and thus the application of counseling techniques becomes haphazard. It is critical for counselors to set limits on their services and on themselves in order to avoid client disappointment and frustration, and in order to avoid getting themselves caught in an impasse that will lead to failure. Counselors who are uncertain as to whether they should be generalists or specialists need to clarify their role and be clear in how they present themselves to clients.

Indeterminate Philosophical Base

Another common obstacle encountered in counseling is the lack of a philosophical base on which counseling goals, objectives, and strategies are built. Counselors who initiate a helping relationship without understanding that their approach and their techniques reflect certain philosophical preferences are indicating their naivete regarding the dynamics of human behavioral change. Whether we are aware of it or not, the way we respond to people, and the opinions, values, choices, or decisions we make are embedded in a philosophical base (Johnson & Vestermark, 1970). It is important for counselors to have an understanding of their own philosophical orientations in order to give direction to counseling. Counselors who involve themselves in helping people make choices, change behavior, and examine the elements that involve personal growth and development must first have done these for themselves. Failure to do so is an acknowledgment of hypocrisy (Barclay, 1968).

What actually occurs in counseling should be related to a counselor's theoretical position on counseling. This should stem from an understanding of the philosophical systems from which a theory of counseling emerges and should be consistently represented in one's style, approach, and technique. Developing a personal theory of counseling is a necessity and should be a focus of any counselor training program. A personal theory of counseling serves to translate philosophical principles into a working format that the counselor can use to guide him or her in the counseling process. Without a theory of counseling, there can be no consistent basis for hypotheses concerning what one's objectives are, and thus counseling becomes a hit-or-miss process. Without a means of identifying what one hopes to accomplish or without a way of consistently measuring it, one cannot determine why counseling has been either effective or ineffective.

Developing a working theory of counseling that stems from an application of philosophical principles is a critical task for all counselors. It is a process that begins by identifying with an orientation with which he or she feels comfortable and modifying it through experience (Stefflre, 1965). A personal theory of counseling should be consistent but flexible and should be continually evaluated as needs, conditions, and experience change (Johnson & Vestermark, 1970). In developing a personal theory of counseling, Blocher (1966, pp. 40-41) suggests several questions a counselor may ask himself:

1. How does the theory deal with the process of human development?
2. How does the theory explain the nature of human learning?
3. How does the theory deal with individual differences?
4. Does the theory offer some central set of constructs or principles for organizing and explaining behavior?
5. How does the theory provide a rationale for counselor behavior?
6. How well does the theory offer possibilities for empirical testing and modification?
7. Is the counseling role implied by this theory one that I can assume?
8. Are the techniques and understandings required by this approach ones that I can master?
9. Are the goals recommended by this theory ones with which I can comfortably identify?

Counselors who have dealt with these or related questions before entering a counseling relationship have a better chance for success with their clients as they will then have a conceptual framework from which to proceed. Counselors with an indeterminate philosophical base will have difficulty in giving direction to the process and in evaluating what is accomplished in counseling.

Counselor Encapsulation

Another frequently encountered barrier to counseling is encapsulation. This refers to the attitudes, values, or beliefs to which counselors cling in order to protect themselves from change. It involves the maintenance of a closed system in terms of interpreting people and events so that openness to change is unlikely. Prejudice, dogmatism, and tunnel vision are part of encapsulation. Viewing all alcoholics as the same, assuming that certain treatment strategies are appropriate for everyone, imposing value judgments on clients, and clinging to outmoded beliefs and methods are some further examples of encapsulation. Encapsulation provides a sense of false security in a rapidly changing world and is a major contributing factor to counselor stagnation. If counselors exhibit behaviors that are resistant to change, rigid, and nonadaptive, they are likely to have difficulty in helping clients change to meet the demands of present realities.

There are many theories, viewpoints, and approaches regarding the treatment of alcoholics which involve a great deal of emotional investment on the part of the therapist. The counselor's reluctance to take a step away from his/her preference and admit that new knowledge, discoveries, and points of view may require changes in what he or she once regarded as enduring truth is an indication of counselor encapsulation. Overreliance upon one's own experience as a frame of reference from which to view clients is a common error made by counselors. Counselors who view alcoholism from a particular perspective that stems from personal experience or training background can easily lose sight of a client's individuality and uniqueness.

In order to avoid the obstacle of encapsulation, counselors must be continually growing, evaluating personal attitudes, values, and experiences, and resisting rigidity in any form. Becoming encapsulated in attitude or behavior is safe and comfortable, but safety and comfort are luxuries foreign to the experience of people involved in the dynamics of helping other people change and grow. Counseling is a journey in personal growth that requires courage, risk, self-awareness, and adaptiveness on the part of the counselor if the process is to have meaning for the client.

Counselor Overinvolvement

Another obstacle found in counseling occurs when counselors become over-involved and cannot detach themselves from their clients. Many beginning counselors feel so responsible for helping clients deal with problems that they lose objectivity and find themselves attempting to rescue clients. There exists a natural tendency to want to protect another person from experiencing hurt or pain, especially after a relationship has been established. However, counselors must always keep in mind that they are professionals, and that in order to be effective, they need to maintain a degree of detachment and objectivity. Being too directive at the wrong time, giving premature. advice, or doing for clients things they should do for themselves are all indicative of over-involvement and loss of perspective.

It is not easy to maintain the necessary warmth, empathy, and caring for clients while still maintaining objectivity, but it is critical to effective counseling. Counselors who have difficulty detaching themselves from their clients' concerns may actually be projecting their own needs onto the relationship. Unrecognized or uncontrolled needs for acceptance and approval may be motivating such counselor behavior. It is also possible that the counselor's personal needs for power and control may cause him or her to become over-involved with clients. In such situations, counselors are attempting to control events to ensure their own success. This is a reflection of an inability to come to terms with one's own limitations and with the idea of possible failure.

Accepting responsibility for one's behavior is a central goal of counseling. Counselors who become over-involved with clients to the point where they have difficulty with detachment keep clients from reaching this goal. If a counselor takes the responsibility for change when it actually belongs to the client, he or she is in danger of fostering an unhealthy dependency and of impairing the client's ability to take responsibility for his or her own actions.

Divided Loyalties

A final obstacle to consider from the counselor's viewpoint is the bind that counselors feel when their loyalties are being pulled in several directions. A counselor has many responsibilities, which include responsibility to the client, to the agency he/she works for, to the alcoholism field, to other professionals, and to society. He or she also may have outside responsibilities involving personal and family commitments. Often these responsibilities are in conflict with one another, and as a result the counselor feels caught in the middle. Counselors report feeling overwhelmed in their attempt to meet obligations to both clients and employers, particularly when one is in conflict with the other. Trying to be all things to all people is an unrealistic expectation, yet many counselors feel such an obligation.

The problem of being torn by multiple commitments is heightened for recovering alcoholic counselors whose previous experience in helping alcoholics has been primarily limited to 12-step work in Alcoholics Anonymous. While such experience has proven to be an asset for developing basic skills for working with people, there is a distinct difference between counseling and 12-step work.

A counselor is a professional and must consider the responsibilities to his/her employer, the agency, the alcoholism field, other colleagues, and to society when he or she provides services to clients. There are limitations on what a counselor can or should do for a client because of his role, whereas in 12-step work he does not have the same considerations. For example, a person doing 12-step work may without reluctance receive phone calls at home from someone troubled by alcohol. However, a counselor must consider his role and the various responsibilities he has. In 12-step work a person is free to act as a friend, but counselors have to place certain limits on their relationships with clients for therapeutic reasons.

These differences are not usually clarified for beginning counselors, who consequently find themselves torn between their loyalty to A.A. and their loyalty to the job. This can become an intensely emotional struggle for the counselor that can eventually hinder effectiveness. It is often peers in A.A. who do not understand a counselor's responsibilities and who may unknowingly place demands upon him that he is unable to meet. It is also possible that the counselor may feel guilty because he finds his work to be so draining that he has little energy left to devote to 12-step work. This can result in criticism from his peers who expect him to devote as much energy to the fellowship as he always has. Occasionally counselors may find it necessary to remind others that they are in A.A. for their own benefit and not there in the capacity of a counselor.

Though it may be forgotten, counselors are people who are bound by the same twenty-four hour day as everyone else and who have limits to their emotional and physical energy. Counseling is demanding and difficult, and because there are multiple commitments pressing upon the counselor, he or she must learn to set priorities within the context of his/her own limitations. In order for a counselor to be effective, he must disentangle himself from nonproductive duties, arrange by order of importance those tasks that are productive, and manage his commitments realistically.

OBSTACLES FOR THE CLIENT

In addition to the obstacles counselors must contend with, there are also factors that hinder clients from contributing to the counseling process. Some of the more common obstacles experienced by clients will be discussed in the following paragraphs, as these can significantly affect the process and outcome of counseling. To be effective, counselors must become aware of these obstacles and guard against their development.

Client Expectations

Johnson and Vestermark (1970) stress the importance of understanding that clients come to counseling with their own beliefs, values, attitudes, and experiences which affect their expectations of the counseling process and their involvement in it. Some clients may expect counselors to tell them what to do and perceive their own role as one of passive recipient. Such a view is reinforced by the traditional approach to health care in which people expect the person charged with the responsibility for healing to somehow do something for them. In counseling, however, recipients of such services are not viewed as patients who have something done to them, but clients who become active participants in the healing process. Counseling is a partnership in which one party facilitates the emergence of growth-producing feelings, thoughts, and behaviors in the other. If counseling is to be effective, responsibility for its results must be shared by the helper and the helpee.

A client's expectations may be entirely accurate, or they may be completely different from what actually occurs. If a client has been in counseling before, he or she is likely to have formed opinions based upon the previous experience. A previously negative experience may have resulted in resentment or disappointment, which is likely to make the client cautious and reserved about entering another counseling experience. His previous experience may make it difficult to trust another counselor, or he may feel so disillusioned that he regards the process as hopeless. Because of the nature of alcoholism, it is probable that a client will have had some previous experience with a counselor or with some form of helping service that is likely to affect his expectational set. Counselors should inquire as to what counseling treatment a client has had and how he views this experience. If it was a negative or neutral experience, counselors will have to devote much time and energy in the early sessions undoing the damage.

Some clients may have had a negative experience but choose to deny it. This presents a more difficult problem for the counselor as the client's resistances are often disguised or are not at the conscious level. Many an impasse in counseling can be traced to an unrecognized expectational set on the part of the client that was not dealt with openly. While there are a variety of ways that clients may indirectly express their negative expectational set, clinical supervision has indicated that behaviors such as missing appointments, arriving late for sessions, not following through on contractual agreements, and avoiding the exploration of threatening areas are some of the common indicators. The tendency in such situations is to work on the specific behavioral indicator, i.e. missing appointments, and to overlook the underlying reason for the behavior. While there certainly can be many reasons for such client behavior, clinical supervision has shown that a frequent factor is the expectational set of the client. Counselors should explore this obstacle with clients by being direct and clear about their realistic or unrealistic expectations of counseling.

When clients have had previously positive experiences with counseling, they are likely to be eager and anticipatory for the counseling process to begin. While one might expect the initial sessions to be easier, the opposite may actually occur. The client may be expecting that counseling this time will be just like it was the last time and be disillusioned, when, for a variety of reasons, it is not the same. He or she may have had warm feelings toward the previous counselor, or have liked the way the program in which he or she was enrolled was conducted, and project these expectations onto this new situation and new counselor. The reality that the new counselor or program is not the same as what he has previously experienced can be disappointing for the client. This may express itself in negativity, avoidance, or resistance behaviors on the part of a client. When this occurs, it is important that counselors recognize that the source for such feelings and behaviors has more to do with the expectations that the client has brought to counseling than what is actually happening between the present counselor and client.

When clients have had no previous experience with counseling, their expectations can be formed by what they have read, by what they have seen or heard on radio or television, or by what their friends may have told them. Often people have the idea that counseling is some mystical process where immediate solutions will be found, or where something magical will occur to solve their problems; or, rather than viewing counseling as a helpful process, some clients influenced by another's opinion may view counseling as repressive and restricting. Certainly, clients who are forced into treatment will view counseling differently from those who seek help of their own accord.

Whether recognized or not, the expectational set of clients highly influences what occurs in counseling. Effective counselors will be aware of the role that these expectations play and will be prepared to deal with them openly and directly. One effective way to do this is to clarify at the very beginning just what counseling is, what the responsibilities of the counselor and client are, what the limits of counseling may be, and what can reasonably be expected from counseling. The expectations that clients have can be an obstacle that seriously hinders the counseling process if it is not recognized and handled appropriately.

Client Ambivalence Toward Change

People who seek help, and even those who are forced to seek counseling help, generally recognize that certain changes in one's feelings, attitudes, or behavior are to be expected. The highly motivated client recognizes the need for change in his or her life, anticipates it, and expects counseling to help in this process. The reluctant and resistant client may not be as cooperative in working with his counselor for this change, but he is generally aware that all is not well and that growth will demand change. Change, even if desired or anticipated, involves fear, anxiety, and apprehension. Even when one's current situation is intolerable, change is frightening because it involves movement from the known to the unknown. Clients are likely to experience an approach-avoidance conflict when they present themselves for counseling, and if not dealt with appropriately by the counselor, this ambivalence toward change can become a major obstacle.

When a client approaches an alcoholism counselor for help, he or she is aware that one of the counselor's goals is to bring the client to an acceptance of his or her alcohol problem, and consequently to change the client's way of viewing and using alcohol. This can be tremendously frightening to someone whose drinking has become so much a part of his life that such a step involves much more than just ceasing to drink. For many, not drinking means an altered life style, changes in social relationships, business practices, family activities, and also one's self-image. There is a great deal of loss experienced by alcoholics who stop drinking. Counselors often minimize the impact of such a loss, and by not processing it thoroughly, can actually help feed into the client's ambivalence toward change. Change, even though growth-promoting and desirable, is often painful. Johnson and Vestermark (1970) identify three stages that must be successfully resolved in dealing with ambivalence toward change: (1) recognizing and accepting the need to change, (2) making the decision to change, and (3) taking action leading to change. These stages will be briefly discussed as they can serve as preliminary guidelines for counselors in dealing with a client's ambivalence to change.

The first challenge for the counselor in working with alcoholics may be the task of helping the client understand and accept his or her alcoholism and consequently the need to change. It is well established that denial is a prevalent defense used by alcoholics, and it represents one of the most difficult barriers in counseling. The person appearing at an alcoholism facility often has his defenses so deeply ingrained that initially most of a counselor's time may be spent on breaking through the denial barrier. To the alcoholic, drinking has become a life-sustaining activity, and it takes a skilled and sensitive counselor to work effectively with a client who categorically denies that he has a problem. An alcoholic who lacks an understanding of the disease process of alcoholism will defend his "right to drink" at all costs. Helping clients recognize their need to change may involve providing information about alcoholism and the disease process such as the physiological effects of alcohol on the body and the psychological and physical aspects of addiction. In addition to the informational or cognitive component, helping an alcoholic recognize and accept his need to change also involves dealing with the emotional and behavioral aspects of drinking. Considering how people drink, when they drink, what happens to them when they drink, what their feelings are before and after drinking, and the effect that the drinking has on those around them are all part of the process involved in recognizing the need to change.

Although one may recognize the need to change, actually making the decision to change is a separate step. Frequently, an alcoholism counselor will have broken through the denial stage to find that the client is still holding onto his or her destructive drinking patterns. The client knows all about the disease, recognizes that he/she has alcoholism, but continues to drink as before. This situation is frustrating for the counselor, but the reality is that recognizing the need to change is only the first step. At this stage, the goal of the counselor is to facilitate the client's decision to change. Two counselor skills are especially important at this point. The ability of the counselor to be *concrete* and his ability to use facilitative *confrontation* are critical helper skills that can be drawn upon to break through this impasse. Clients will often attempt to be vague, abstract, and general in their expressions in order to avoid making a decision to change. It is as if they have intellectually accepted their alcoholism but have not yet integrated this knowledge with their emotions and their behavior. By being very specific and concrete, counselors can avoid falling into the trap of redundancy which only serves as a further avoidance technique for clients. Using confrontation effectively can also help facilitate a breakthough. By pointing out the discrepancies between what clients say and how they behave, counselors are helping the client toward a decision to change. Confrontation can be an extremely effective skill when used at the right time and in the right manner, but it can also be destructive. Confrontation may help or hinder the counseling process, and because of the power it has to do either, it will be discussed in more detail in a later chapter. Unless the decision to change is a firm commitment, real change will not occur. Confrontation and concreteness are two counselor skills that can help clients go beyond simply recognizing their need to change to actually making a decision.

The third stage in overcoming client ambivalence toward change is taking *action* steps for change. In some cases, clients may recognize their need for change, make a decision to change, and then not follow through with concrete action. It may be that the fear becomes overwhelming or that the client begins to doubt his or her resources for adjusting to the change. He/she may just give up. The real test of a counselor's effectiveness comes at this stage, as it is here that clients will either break through their ambivalence and begin taking the necessary steps to reach their goal, or they will remain caught in the destructive pattern of desiring change but being unable to act upon it. If this occurs, the client's self-image deteriorates, his motivation diminishes, and hopelessness sets in. The counselor's support and leadership are needed now more than ever to help the client take the painful steps involved in changing behavior.

Many clients recognize their need to change and decide that they will change, but become frustrated because they just do not know how to change. It is at this point that counselors can fall short by assuming that just because clients decide to change that somehow they will. The reality is that clients often do not know how to change and look to the counselor to teach them the "how to" steps. It is easy to forget that when clients come for help they are in crisis and as a result may not be able to function normally. Going to an A.A. meeting may be an agreed-upon decision, but many clients never make it because they are too embarrassed to ask "simple" questions about how to get there or what to expect when they do get there. Counselors who do not check out the action steps to make sure the client knows what to do to reach his/her goal are not doing their job. Taking the client through the desired action steps is as much a part of effective counseling as is understanding and empathy. Developing simple, systematic steps to reach a desired goal, building in reinforcements that reward clients when they make progress in achieving their goal, and developing feedback procedures to evaluate the action steps being taken are all part of the change process.

A commitment to change means vulnerability. The obstacles to effective counseling that stem from the client's ambivalence to change are great; however, they also involve the potential for making the change process meaningful and progressive. For each step involved in change, the counselor's action is critical in setting the stage for constructive, growth-producing change.

Client Manipulations

Clients can engage in several manipulative strategies to avoid change. Client manipulations may be conscious or unconscious and can be an obstacle to effective counseling if the counselor remains unaware of what is happening. Most clients want relief from their problems, but because of the anxieties surrounding change, they may attempt to control the counseling relationship. Such attempts serve to maintain an unhealthy safety in the relationship by keeping the counselor from pursuing sensitive areas. The client is often in conflict regarding the use of manipulative strategies because in one respect he or she wants the counselor to deal with those areas that are most painful, but in other respects is fearful of the potential hurt involved in such disclosures. Counselors, in their concern for the client, may unknowingly fall prey to client protection maneuvers, which may be harmful. A frequent manipulative tactic used by clients to accomplish their goal is to place the counselor on the defensive. Clients may continually challenge or defy the counselor, resulting in the counselor having to explain every request, insight, or response made to the client. Clients can also place the counselor in the omnipotent healer role and demand solutions to the problems they are experiencing. "You're the counselor; what am I supposed to do?" is the type of manipulative question indicative of the client's desire to place responsibility for change onto the counselor. By allowing clients to have control of the relationship, counselors allow the focus of attention to shift from the client's concerns to what the counselor is doing, saying, and feeling.

When clients attempt to gain control, it should be recognized that these manipulative tactics are defensive behaviors. It is as if the relationship is being tested to see if the counselor is strong enough not to allow the client to be successful in behaviors that are self-defeating. "Is the counselor aware enough to not allow me success in those tactics I use with everyone else? Is he good enough to set limits on the relationship so that I am not permitted to be less than what I can be? Is this counselor worthy of my trust and deserving of my confidence?" Such questions lie behind the manipulative strategies that clients often use to gain acceptance and security. Clients want to know if a counselor is going to be any different from other people in their lives and will play games in order to find out. Other manipulations may involve sexual overtures, role stereotypes ("I'm such a sensitive person, please don't hurt me"), or subtle maneuverings relating to the counseling sessions such as constantly being late, missing appointments entirely, or telephoning the counselor inappropriately at home.

Whether manipulative client behaviors are at the conscious or unconscious level, they require careful attention by the counselor. If recognized, confronted directly, and dealt with therapeutically, they can serve as a stimulus for effective counseling rather than an obstacle to constructive change.

Discussion in this chapter has explored some of the more frequent obstacles to effective counseling that come from both the counselor's and the client's perspective. Counseling is a dynamic human encounter in which subtleties of interpersonal interaction cannot be ignored. As Carl Rogers has pointed out (1962, p. 416), "The quality of the personal encounter is probably, in the long run, the element which determines the extent to which this [counseling] is an experience which releases or promotes development and growth." The counselor needs to be aware of what he or she and the client bring to the counseling situation, what they expect of and from it, and how their interaction can either hinder or facilitate a productive relationship. In discussing some of the more common obstacles encountered in counseling, it is hoped that the reader will not be overly concerned or anxious, but rather that counselors will have a greater awareness of themselves, their clients, and the counseling process and thus be better equipped to do an effective job. In providing some cautions, checkpoints, and guidelines, it is hoped that the alcoholism counselor will have more confidence in himself and in the process to which he is dedicated.

Chapter 9

SUPERVISION

O NE of the most significant factors involved in becoming an effective counselor is supervision. Supervision provides the opportunity for a counselor to relate his hopes, struggles, aspirations, disappointments, failures, and growth to another person. It serves as a resource for counselors to evaluate the what, how, and why of the counseling process in a manner that facilitates growth for themselves and ultimately for their clients.

Supervision is a necessary ingredient in the development of an effective alcoholism counselor. It is, however, a concept that has various meanings, depending upon the context in which it occurs and the expectations of the supervisor and the supervisee. Unfortunately, supervision for alcoholism counselors is often fragmented, vague or nonexistent. Since this condition is a disservice to counselors and to clients as well, an attempt will be made to clarify the ambiguity surrounding the meaning of supervision by providing a conceptual understanding of the term, by providing an understanding of various supervisory methods and procedures, and by identifying some of the critical variables involved.

Competent and continuous supervision for alcoholism counselors is both a right and a necessity. It is a matter of questionable ethics for a counselor to assume the responsibilities of counseling without having experienced adequate supervision during training as well as continuous on-the-job supervision. It may also be argued that administrators who fail to provide resources for adequate supervision of counselors are irresponsible in their management of clinical services. Programs are obligated to provide supervision to maintain quality care, and counselors have a right to expect it.

Although supervision is a term familiar to most helpers, its precise meaning is difficult to define. Confusion regarding the meaning of supervision results from different uses of the term in different settings. For some, supervision implies a superior-subordinate relationship as defined by one's position in an organizational structure. Others regard supervision as an equalitarian relationship where advice is sought and the decision to accept or reject the advice is left to the helper. Some regard supervision as focusing primarily on issues regarding the efficient management of responsibilities, while others view the process as enabling the supervisee to be more effective in the performance of duties. Supervision can also be viewed as a highly structured process with roles and expectations clearly defined, or as an experiential process.

The confusion regarding supervision is understandable in the context of its historical development as an ingredient of helping relationships. Supervision as understood by the medical, social work, and psychology professions will briefly be considered in the following paragraphs. From this will emerge a conceptual framework for a model of supervision in alcoholism counseling.

The medical model of supervision can historically be traced to the development of medical school training which included both clinical and classroom instruction. Clinical instruction of students by outstanding practitioners has been an integral part of medical education. Although this instruction is referred to as supervision, it is essentially an educational process where the main objective is the student's education (Kutzik, 1977). The traditional relationship of interns and residents to their clinical instructors in teaching hospitals is, however, also supervisory. The supervision of residents and interns includes administrative as well as educational components by nature of the organizational hierarchy of teaching hospitals. Thus, the medical model of supervision involves both educational and administrative functions that are time-limited (Kutzik, 1977).

The emergence of the social work field into an autonomous profession has seen the function of supervision change with the growth of the profession. During different periods in the history of social work, supervision was viewed as having administrative, educational, supportive, consultative, and therapeutic functions (Kadushin, 1976). The administrative aspect of supervision placed emphasis upon overseeing and monitoring the activities of supervisees. The educational aspect emphasized the transmission of information, knowledge, and skills to supervisees. The focus was on teaching the social work trainee how to do his job while providing the necessary support to enable him to learn from experience. As the profession developed, supervision moved away from the administrative, supportive, and educational models towards one in which supervision was viewed as helping supervisees resolve personal or emotional problems. Although this "pseudo-therapy" concept of supervision (Marcus, 1927) provided a means for supervisees to process personal limitations interfering with job performance, it served a limited function. The more predominant and the most current conception of supervision in social work practice places emphasis upon its consultative functions. Defining the supervisor as a consultant emphasizes the advisory and collaborative function rather than the superior-subordinate one. This concept of the supervisor is based upon one's expertise rather than one's ascribed authority. The supervisor is one who has prestige by virtue of the knowledge, skill, and expertise he/she possesses (Vinter, 1959).

Recently the National Association of Social Workers has attempted to clarify the concept of supervision in terms of the different roles and levels of social work personnel (NASW, 1973). Essentially, it regards the supervision of social workers as moving from close supervision for those with limited training to consultation for those with advanced training and credentials. Social workers with associate or bachelor degrees receive close supervision which includes administrative supervision. Those with graduate degrees or further training receive less supervision with more emphasis placed upon collaborative consultation with colleagues.

Supervision as perceived from a psychological model can be viewed in terms of three major approaches. Counselor supervision has different emphasis depending upon whether the counselor is being supervised from a psychotherapeutic, behavioral, or integrative approach (Boyd, 1978). These three approaches will be briefly explained to provide an overview of counselor supervision from a psychological framework.

There is strong support for the view that counselor supervision is similar to counseling and psychotherapy (Altucher, 1967; Arbuckle, 1965; Boyd, 1978; Kell & Mueller, 1966; Mueller & Kell, 1972; Patterson, 1964). The psychotherapeutic approach to counselor supervision focuses upon the intrapersonal and interpersonal dynamics of the counseling relationship. A basic assumption in this approach is that counseling is, in part, an emotional experience, and the processing of the intrapersonal and interpersonal dynamics is a crucial aspect of supervision. The counselor needs to be aware of these dynamics and of how he or she can utilize them to induce therapeutic change (Boyd, 1978). The goal of psychotherapeutic supervision is for counselors to learn what is therapeutic and how to function in a therapeutic manner (Mueller & Kell, 1972). This involves becoming aware of intrapersonal and interpersonal dynamics, understanding the effect of these dynamics on the helping relationship, changing these dynamics, and learning how to utilize these dynamics for therapeutic gain (Boyd, 1978).

There are adaptions of the psychotherapeutic approach to supervision which differ in degree rather than kind. For example, the classic approach to psychotherapeutic supervision focuses upon the client's defensive patterns and the therapist's counter-transference problems. The emphasis is on the client's or the therapist's pathology and understanding the interaction that occurs (Abroms, 1977). The concept of metatherapy also is an adaption of the psychotherapeutic approach to supervision. This concept views supervision as a therapy of therapy where the focus is upon the therapist-client relationship. It is conceptually similar to family therapy where the client is not a simple family member but rather the family's relationship system. Thus, supervision as metatherapy is a relationship between a supervisor and a therapeutic relationship (Abroms, 1977).

While there are variations within psychotherapeutic approaches to supervision, they are similar in their focus on relationship dynamics. The process by which this form of supervision occurs is usually unstructured in order to emphasize the dynamics of interactions between counselor and client or counselor and supervisor. When this develops into therapy for the counselor, it emphasizes the processing of those dynamics that relate to the counselor's performance.

A second major approach to counselor supervision from the psychological perspective is the behavioral approach. The focus of the behavioral approach to counselor supervision is upon teaching counseling skills to supervisees and learning to extinguish inappropriate behaviors. It is based upon the assumption that counseling skills can be behaviorally defined, measured, and taught by methods based upon psychological learning theory. Behavioral supervision is specific in nature as it focuses upon individual skill level and teaches supervisees how to increase their skill level. The process of behavioral supervision involves five steps (Boyd, 1978): (1) establishment of a relationship between the supervisor and counselor, (2) assessment of the counselor's skill level, (3) setting of supervision goals, (4) development and implementation of strategies to meet these goals, and (5) evaluation of the learning.

In the psychotherapeutic approach, the supervisor-counselor relationship is the primary source of learning, but in the behavioral approach it is only part of the process. Once a facilitative relationship has been established, the focus is upon evaluating each skill and then establishing learning goals to increase the counselor's performance in these skills. Assessment of a counselor's skills enables supervision goals to be selected. For these goals to have meaning, they must be selected by both the counselor and the supervisor and also be behaviorally specific. The counselor and supervisor then develop problem-solving strategies as to how these specific goals can be reached and, when attained, how they can be evaluated. Some of the more common methods used by behavioral supervisors are modeling, reinforcement, role-playing, and microcounseling.

The integrative approaches to counselor supervision include those that combine aspects from several supervisory approaches (Boyd, 1978). In fact, most supervisors borrow from several modalities and merge them with their own style. The most conceptually developed integrative approach to counselor supervision combining the elements of a psychotherapeutic and a behavioral approach is the Carkhuff Supervisory Training Model.

The Carkhuff Training Model (*see* Chap. 4, "A Helping Model for Alcoholism Counselors") is perhaps the most well-known and thoroughly researched helping and supervisory model (Carkhuff, 1969; Carkhuff & Berenson, 1976, 1977; Carkhuff & Truax, 1965). It is based on a theory of helping that involves the counselor responsive conditions of empathy, positive regard or respect, genuineness, and concreteness and the counselor initiative dimensions of confrontation, immediacy, and other action-oriented skills including problem-solving and program development skills. The counselor responsive dimensions guide the helpee through a self-exploration and self-understanding learning process which prepares the client for the initiative dimensions that in turn encourages helpee directionality and construction action. The emphasis in supervision is to teach counselors how to offer high levels of both the responsive and action-oriented conditions. This is accomplished through discrimination training, communication training, and training in developing effective courses of action. In discrimination training, the emphasis is on learning to distinguish helpful from unhelpful counselor responses. The focus of communication training is to increase a counselor's responsive skills to at least minimally effective levels. In training for developing effective courses of action, the emphasis is on developing a repertoire of systematic action-oriented skills and applying "preferred modes of treatment" to encourage helpees to take specific action. The Carkhuff Supervisory Training Model integrates experiential, didactic, and modeling methods of learning in the pursuit of these goals.

SUPERVISION IN ALCOHOLISM COUNSELING

The perspectives and experiences of the medical, social work, and psychology professions can be drawn upon in formulating a conceptual model of supervision for alcoholism counseling. Supervision is a vague term in alcoholism services because its meaning depends upon the setting and the training levels of supervisors and supervisees. In many alcoholism programs, the supervisor is the director. If his or her background is primarily administrative, supervision is likely to be perceived in terms of monitoring staff from a management perspective. In other alcoholism settings, the person responsible for supervising counselors may be an advanced counselor who has had some experience and training in working with alcoholics. Such supervisors are likely to adopt a teaching or instructional set in their supervision of counselors. In settings where alcoholism services are part of a larger mental health component, supervision of alcoholism counselors is likely to come from persons of other professional disciplines such as psychiatry, psychology, or social work. Such settings place greater emphasis upon formal credentials and regard the supervisory process as primarily clinical in nature. Many counselors are recovering alcoholics who have not been formally trained in counseling, while others may have formal counseling education but limited experience in alcoholism. Because alcoholism counselors have such diverse experience and training, it would be expected that a supervision model would reflect this variability.

The supervision of alcoholism counselors can be viewed as having three components to ensure the efficiency and effectiveness of a counselor's work. These components include managerial, educational, and clinical functions. Counselors need to be supervised in light of administrative expectations concerning the responsibilities they have to the community, the profession, and funding resources. Supervisors need to be concerned with the efficiency of a counselor's work. For example, making sure counselors keep appointments, complete records, honor obligations, conduct themselves in a professional manner, and contribute to harmony among colleagues is a supervisory concern that is administrative in nature. Because many counselors learn about counseling on the job, supervision also needs to involve instruction. Teaching counselors about such areas as human development, counseling methods and techniques, principles of abnormal psychology, and the physiological, psychological, and cultural factors of alcoholism is a supervisory function.

Counselors need to be continually expanding their knowledge in order to maintain their effectiveness. Supervision emphasizing teaching and education is one way to accomplish this.

A third function of alcoholism counselors supervision is clinical in nature. Without adequate clinical supervision, counselors are likely to flounder and never develop their potential. Clinical supervision involves focusing upon counselor and client interactions, as well as dealing with the problems encountered in counseling. It should be separated from managerial and educational supervision so that the counselor feels free to disclose one's thoughts without concern for one's position in the organization. The primary focus of clinical supervision is to help counselors become more effective therapists. To do so, counselors must be free from performance anxiety or the fear of being reprimanded. A counselor receiving clinical supervision needs to focus entirely on what is happening in counseling with respect to the client, the counselor, and the client-counselor relationship.

What is being suggested here is a model of supervision that has three distinct functions which improve a counselor's efficiency and effectiveness. The efficiency of a counselor depends upon the nature and extent of administrative supervision received, while his or her effectiveness is related to the quality of educational and clinical supervision. All three components are necessary, though it is unlikely that one supervisor will carry out all three functions. Because alcoholism services are so diversified, it is best for each program to design the specific manner in which this supervision is provided. From an administrative, educational, and clinical perspective, adequate supervision is essential to maintain quality services and should be available as a resource for counselor development.

CLINICAL PRECEPTORSHIP: A MODEL FOR CLINICAL SUPERVISION

Recognizing that alcoholism counselors rarely have the opportunity to receive clinical supervision (Powell, 1976), the Eastern Area Alcohol Education and Training Program, Inc., has developed a unique and innovative approach for meeting the need of this form of supervision. Counselors recognize the need to develop their clinical skills beyond what is learned at training workshops, seminars, or schools of alcohol studies. While these resources provide a valuable function in the professional development of alcoholism counselors, they are not a substitute for the learning that occurs in actual practice. For this learning to be constructive, there must be a means through which counselors can process these experiences in a nonjudgmental, supportive, and facilitative atmosphere. The clinical preceptorship program is one way in which alcoholism counselors can pursue these goals. One of the advantages of the clinical preceptorship program is the provision of a vehicle for counselors to receive clinical supervision without having to go to the expense and time of attending workshops that take a counselor out of the office. It is also structured to provide frequent and ongoing supervision which fosters continuity and commitment to professional skill development.

The preceptorship program is a clinical supervisory model that provides an opportunity for intense, one-to-one or small group clinical supervision of alcoholism counselors (E.A.A.E.T.P., 1978). The purposes of the preceptorship program are as follows:

1. Provide an advanced form of clinical training that assesses the clinical skills of alcoholism counselors.
2. Develop counselor skills by providing continuous feedback regarding the approaches, strategies, techniques, and assumptions operating in counseling.
3. Constructively impact the profession of alcoholism counseling by increasing job satisfaction and decreasing those factors that contribute to turnover, burn-out, and low morale.
4. Identify counselor's strengths and weaknesses by means of a monitoring and evaluation system that is based upon emotional support, confidentiality, and mutual trust.
5. Constructively affect the quality of client care by increasing the clinical competence of those charged with the responsibility of counseling.

Clinical supervision in this model is viewed as a tutorial process whereby the principles and processes of counseling are developed into practical skills. The preceptor (clinical supervisor) is viewed as both an educator and coach who focuses upon the current level of a counselor's skills while helping to increase these skills. It is an intense, personalized, and individual process that utilizes such methods as case reviews, verbatims, and direct or indirect observations of counseling sessions.

A preceptor is an accomplished clinician who, by successfully surviving a rigorous selection procedure, is recognized by the E.A.A.E.T.P. as being professionally qualified to provide clinical supervision to alcoholism counselors. A preceptor must meet the following requirements:

1. The person must have a minimum of five years experience as a clinician, with two of the five years as a clinical supervisor.
2. Two of the five years are to have been spent working with a caseload in which at least 50 percent of the clients were alcoholics.
3. He must have a minimum of three years approved, full-time clinical supervision in the practice of counseling.
4. The preceptor must be familiar with recent developments in the alcohol field.
5. The clinical preceptor must possess at least a master's degree in a relevant behavioral science field or have equivalent stature in the field as determined by the E.A.A.E.T.P. Accreditation and Clinical Training Committee.
6. The preceptor must be a practicing clinician of either a full-time, part-time, or private practice nature.
7. The individual must have made a significant contribution to the field of alcoholism, with a demonstrated advanced level of clinical competence and experience as determined by the E.A.A.E.T.P. Accreditation and Clinical Training Committee.
8. The clinical preceptor is required to have a screening interview with the E.A.A.E.T.P. Accreditation and Clin-

ical Training Committee. The preceptor may be requested to submit a case analysis and description as part of the application process.

If a preceptor meets the above qualifications and is approved by the E.A.A.E.T.P., an agreement is reached that specifies the responsibilities of all parties involved. Agencies or individuals may then make arrangements with the E.A.A.E.T.P. for a preceptor to provide clinical supervision to alcoholism counselors. The supervision proceeds according to individualized parameters agreed upon by the agency, the counselor, the preceptor, and the E.A.A.E.T.P. While there is flexibility for individual preferences, the process is always continuous, personalized, and intensive in nature. Because the preceptor does not have daily supervisory responsibility for counselors, but limits his involvement solely to clinical issues, there is greater potential for beneficial results. It is a program that addresses itself to the unique needs of a growing profession in an innovative and creative manner.

METHODS OF SUPERVISION

Some of the methods supervisors of alcoholism counselors can use in implementing a supervisory model will be the focus of this section. These methods have been drawn from several approaches and represent some of the more innovative and effective supervisory strategies reported in the literature. Rather than suggesting one method for alcoholism counseling, several will be presented. It is suggested that supervisors draw from several of these in formulating the strategies most relevant for supervising alcoholism counselors.

The most common methods of supervision have historically relied upon one-to-one interaction and the case-conference methods. In one-to-one supervision, the counselor typically presents a progress report and then processes specific cases with the supervisor. The direction of one-to-one supervision depends to a great extent upon the approach of the supervisor. For example, a supervisor who stresses the psychotherapeutic approach will focus upon the dynamic elements of the client-counselor and supervisor-counselor relationship, whereas a behaviorally oriented supervisor will focus more on the specific skills of counseling. While the approaches to one-to-one supervision can vary, the method is always intense and individualized. Because the demand for one-to-one supervision far outnumbers the availability of supervisors, individual clinical supervision is not often practical. The case-conference method is a traditional approach to supervision that is applied in settings where individual sessions are not feasible. The case-conference is a process of consultation where a counselor presents a case to a professional staff for the purpose of sharing knowledge and skills. Rather than individualized discussions of cases, supervision by this method becomes a group process with input from several staff members. While both of these methods have merit, more specific and creative methods of supervision have been recently introduced. The methods that will be presented in this section include microtraining, interpersonal process recall, co-therapy, peer-group supervision, and role-playing.

Microtraining

Microtraining is a systematic approach to counselor-skill development whereby specific skills are practiced, monitored by videotape, and evaluated, and feedback is given regarding the level of skill attainment. Microtraining has been successfully applied in teaching counseling skills in a variety of settings (Bellucci, 1972; Boyd, 1973; Ivey, 1971). The microtraining program developed by Ivey (1971) has received wide acceptance as a successful method of counselor training and supervision. There are essentially nine steps to this method (Ivey, 1971):

1. A trainee attempts to perform a specific skill.
2. This attempt is videotaped.
3. An evaluation of the skill is obtained.
4. The trainee then reads a manual describing the skill to be learned.
5. An expert demonstrates the skill through videotape.
6. The videotaped performance is critiqued by the trainee

and the supervisor.

7. The trainee and supervisor prepare for another performance of the skill.
8. A second attempt of the skill is videotaped.
9. Feedback and evaluation are given to the trainee.

Microtraining incorporates the learning principles of feedback, reinforcement, and shaping and is a highly successful method of supervision (Boyd, 1978). It provides the framework to enable counselors to learn one skill at a time while providing feedback on their strengths and weaknesses. Seeing an expert model the skill demonstrates that the skill can be learned and encourages trainees to practice. While there are obvious advantages to videotape, the same nine-step model can be adapted to audiotape or other means of direct or indirect observation.

Interpersonal Process Recall

The interpersonal process recall procedure was initially developed by Kagan and Krathwohl (1967) and has received considerable attention in the professional literature on counselor education and training (Archer & Kagan, 1973; Kagan & Schauble, 1969; Spivack, 1970). The method uses recorded playbacks of counseling interactions to help counselors identify and recall dynamics which may have interfered with effective communication. The purpose is to increase the counselor's awareness of the feelings and thoughts that have affected the counseling session. The playback is combined with inductive questioning by the supervisor to focus upon the intrapersonal and interpersonal dynamics that are operating. Examples of questions which a supervisor may use to elicit responses are as follows (Dendy, 1971):

1. What do you think the client was trying to say?
2. What do you think the client was feeling at this point?
3. What was going on in your mind when the client said that?
4. Can you recall some of the feelings you were having?

5. If you had another chance, would you like to have said something different?

The principle objectives of interpersonal process recall supervision are to —

1. Assist the counselor to see himself as he really is.
2. Help the counselor to understand himself, his feelings, his thoughts, and the reasons for his behavior.
3. Increase counselor awareness of verbal and nonverbal communication between himself and his client.

In supervision by the interpersonal process recall method, recall can also be applied to clients, with the counselor observing the client's participation in the recall process. This helps counselors become aware of the subtle variation in meanings between client's verbal and nonverbal behavior. Mutual recall can also be applied where the counselor and client share their recall with one another as they listen to the playback.

Interpersonal process recall has been reported to be successful as a method for enhancing counselor effectiveness and client progress (Kagan et al., 1963; Kagan & Schauble, 1969). It is most effective using videotape playback. However, good results have been reported with audiotape as well. The methodology of interpersonal process recall supervision requires supervisors to possess advanced clinical skills and should thus be applied in settings where skilled supervisors are available.

Co-therapy

Another method by which counselors may develop their skills and learn more about the therapeutic process is cotherapy. This occurs when a supervisor and counselor see clients together, thus sharing clinical responsibility. This provides the opportunity for counselors to develop confidence as they both participate and observe. Counselors using this method can receive direct feedback on their work and take more risks, knowing that an experienced therapist is present. It also reduces the sense of being overwhelmed with the responsibilities of counseling and demystifies the process.

There are difficulties encountered in using co-therapy as a supervisory method. The relationship between the supervisor and counselor may not be therapeutically compatible and may thus restrain the counselor from involvement. The counselor may also be overly concerned with trying to please the supervisor to the extent that attention is drawn away from the client. Communication between the supervisor and counselor is critical to this method, particularly since the results of poor communication are likely to affect the client. There may also be underlying competitive feelings which hinder the counseling process. Despite the difficulties involved in co-therapy, the potential benefits to the counselor and the client far outweigh the disadvantages. For co-therapy to be successful, a great deal of openness, sensitivity, and frank communication between the supervisor and counselor are required. Structured appropriately, it is an effective supervisory method (Abroms, 1977).

Peer Group Supervision

In many settings, there is minimal opportunity for supervision due to the unavailability of adequately trained supervisors or the lack of funding. When it is impractical or impossible to have the resources of a specific supervisor, peer supervision is a creative way to provide for the advantages of supervision. Effective counselors are constantly learning and growing. There is benefit to sharing these learning experiences with peers. While peer supervision should not be regarded as a substitute for a supervisor, it can serve as an effective supplement (Freleigh & Buchheimer, 1969). A peer supervisor is a counselor who is on administrative and clinical parity with other counselors but who accepts a supervisory role specific to the supervision session. The primary role for the peer supervisor is to facilitate feedback and sharing among the counselors. Emphasis is placed upon skill awareness and reinforcement, with evaluative functions being de-emphasized. Freleigh and Buchheimer (1969) suggest three factors that determine the effectiveness of peer supervision: the attitude of the peer supervisor, the format of peer supervision, and training in peer supervision. A helpful, cooperative attitude that does not present an air of superiority is crucial in effective peer supervision. The format should be structured yet flexible and should stress feedback and reinforcement. It is also important for peer supervisors to be trained in the process before initiating a peer supervisory session.

Peer supervision has been recognized as contributing to the supervisory process and can be utilized in a variety of alcohol treatment settings. It has its limits, but with adequate preparation and structure, it can be a valuable learning method.

Role-Playing

There is considerable evidence that supports the efficacy of role-playing as a valuable method in counselor education and training (Eisenberg & Delaney, 1970; Kaslow et al., 1977; Mann & Mann, 1966). Supervisors can utilize role-playing exercises in a number of creative ways to facilitate counselor learning. By acting in the role of helpee, counselors experience the impact of being on the receiving end of a helping relationship. This helps to sensitize counselors to the emotional struggles of clients. Specific incidences in therapy can be role-played in supervision to help counselors process the experience and to gain new insight when approaching similar situations. Role playing exercises can be designed to prepare counselors by practicing some of the situations frequently encountered in counseling. For example, how to deal with silence, client manipulation, or transference and counter-transference problems can be practiced effectively before a counselor experiences them in a counseling session. The use of role-playing as a therapeutic technique can also be experimented with in a supervisory session.

The effectiveness of a counselor depends upon the extent of his/her growth as a person and as a professional. Supervision is one of the primary means to insure counselor growth. This chapter advocates direct, continuous, and intensive supervision for alcoholism counselors as both a professional right and a necessity. Three components of alcoholism counselor supervision have been presented, all of which need to be provided. The management supervisory function is important to maintain counselor efficiency, while education and clinical functions are necessary for counselor effectiveness. The preceptorship program, an effective model for clinical supervision of alcoholism counselors, has been presented, as have several supervisory methods.

Chapter 10

SIGNIFICANT TREATMENT ISSUES

THIS chapter will examine three of the most significant treatment issues in counseling alcoholic people. There are many issues that present problems for counselors in the course of treating alcoholics, some of which are dealt with in other chapters. There are, however, three issues that consistently emerge as factors counselors have difficulty with and which significantly affect the results of counseling. Confrontation, the first issue covered in this chapter, is one of the most used and abused counseling techniques. It is a powerful treatment tool, but its effects can be for better or worse. Counseling the reluctant and resistant client is the second issue covered in this chapter. Perhaps no problem is so prevalent for alcoholism counselors than learning how to work with clients who do not want help or who resist it. The third issue considered in this chapter is termination. Terminating counseling effectively is a critical but often neglected treatment variable. It is as important to constructive counseling as establishing a meaningful relationship with clients.

CONFRONTATION: FOR BETTER OR WORSE

Excerpts from clinical sessions with alcoholic clients indicate a reliance upon confrontation as a therapeutic tool in motivating clients to change. Counselors in clinical settings are urged to confront clients about their behavior as a means of breaking through the denial pattern (Clinebell, 1968); industrial counselors and supervisors are encouraged to confront employees about their job performance (Phillips & Older, 1977); counselors working with families are advised to utilize confrontation as a technique for initiating family intervention (Howard & Howard, 1976; Johnson, 1973). While it is assumed that confrontation is an effective technique in alcoholism counseling, in terms of recent research evidence there appears to have been little thought given to the complexities of confrontation as a change variable. Confrontation is applied in a variety of counseling situations and at various intensity levels, depending upon the actual setting and the individual counselor's discretion. There does not, however, seem to be a conceptual understanding of where and how confrontation should be used, nor an appreciation for the potentially negative impact inappropriate confrontations can have upon clients. The use of confrontation can be a haphazard technique, serving more as a barometer of the counselor's frustration than as a skill for facilitating constructive client change.

Confrontation is one of the most powerful dimensions in helping relationships with the potential for having extremely positive or negative results (Berenson & Mitchell, 1974). This section will review recent research regarding confrontation and develop a perspective from which to view its application. Confrontation can add a dynamic dimension to a counselor's repertoire of helping skills. In the hand of a counselor with limited skills, confrontation becomes a vehicle for irresponsible venting of frustration and hostility.

Traditional schools of counseling and psychotherapy have stressed either a warm, passive, accepting role for the counselor or a more detached, aloof, and analytic one. More recently, counselors have been encouraged to confront clients as well as the "system," whether it be a government bureaucracy, business, or significant people in the client's life. Advocates for confrontation in counseling have influenced such specific therapeutic approaches as encounter groups, sensitivity training, assertiveness training, and other specialized techniques (Bower & Bower, 1976; Dyer, 1972; Yalom, 1970). The philosophical foundation of many treatment centers is based upon confrontation (Guy, 1968), despite the lack of evidence supporting the efficacy of using confrontation as a basis for facilitating constructive change in clients (Berenson & Mitchell, 1974; Carkhuff, 1969; Muchowski & Valle, 1977).

The focus of this section is to demonstrate that while confrontation may have certain contributory functions in certain counseling relationships, confrontation is never necessary or sufficient. If a counselor takes the time to understand a client, then through this understanding he or she should be able to accomplish anything that a confrontation would (Berenson & Mitchell, 1974). However, many alcoholism counselors find themselves in crisis situations where time is a luxury they do not have. In cases of time-limited intervention, confrontation may be effective if used by counselors who have earned the right to help on the basis of the helping skills they have mastered (Carkhuff, 1969, 1971). Confrontation, then, is never necessary or sufficient in and of itself, but it may be efficient (Berenson & Mitchell, 1974).

When used by highly skilled helpers, confrontation has various functions. It can serve to create a crisis in the helping relationship that will allow the counselor and the client to move to higher levels of understanding. It can also draw the focus of the interaction to the here and now, thereby limiting time spent on irrelevant material. Confrontations that deal with discrepancies in the client's behavior can uncover new areas to explore which may have been subconsciously protected by the helpee. They also can serve as a test of the client's motivation and readiness to take the necessary action steps needed for change. Confrontation does have a function, but whether it is constructive or destructive to the helping process will depend upon the helper's skill in terms of how he or she uses the technique and his sense of when it should be applied.

One of the most definitive and comprehensive publications dealing with confrontation has been developed by Berenson and Mitchell (1974). The research upon which their formulations are based is comprehensive, sufficiently rigorous, and penetratingly meaningful as they place confrontation in perspective.

After years of research on this dimension, Berenson and Mitchell (1974) identify five types of confrontations that have surfaced. The five major types identified through their research are experiential, didactic, strength, weakness, and encouragement to action. Experiential confrontations are those in which the helper responds to discrepancies that he or she perceives in the helping relationship or to discrepancies that the helpee is personally experiencing. When a helpee says one thing overtly but his or her nonverbal behavior is indicative of something else internally, an experiential confrontation may be in order; or perhaps the helpee may indicate how much he values the counseling relationship but may act in ways that are self-contradictory, such as continually missing appointments or arriving late for sessions. In these situations, a helper's confrontation of the discrepancy regarding the helping relationship needs to be initiated and is defined as an experiential confrontation.

Didactic confrontations are those in which the helper attempts to clarify misinformation or the lack of information that the client may have about his problem or his/her interpretation of it. Many alcoholic clients have a limited understanding of their condition or even of how they ended up in treatment. The distortions and myths surrounding alcoholism encourage the use of didactic confrontations to objectively clarify client misconceptions. An analysis of alcoholism counselors' responses to client statements indicated a high percentage of confronting statements, most of which could be categorized as didactic confrontations (Valle, 1978). Apparently alcoholism counselors are more comfortable with confronting clients on informational issues rather than with experiential processes. Strength confrontations are those which focus on the assets or resources of the helpee, and weakness confrontations are those which refer to the helpee's limitations or deficits. The fifth type of confrontation, encouragement to action, involves the helper directing the helpee with specific steps toward change. The focus of these types of confrontations is to help clients realize that they can have an impact on their world by acting rather than by being passive observers.

In addition to specifying the types of confrontations used in counseling, the pioneering work of Berenson and Mitchell (1974) establishes a sequence of confrontations which determine when and where in the helping process they can be effective. They explain this sequence in terms of the helping model developed by Carkhuff (*see* Chap. 4), which views effective helping as a function of both helper and helpee dimensions. The helper dimension includes both responsive and initiative skills which the highly skilled counselor utilizes to facilitate the helpee dimensions of exploration, understanding, and action. Confrontation is a helper-initiated skill that should only be used when the helper has demonstrated that he or she can respond to the helpee at interchangeable and additive levels. Effective confrontation must be based upon a high level of responsiveness to the helpee. This demonstrates the helper's understanding of the helpee and sets the stage for confrontation. To confront without understanding may do more harm than to take no action at all!

During the exploration phase, the helper's focus is upon those responses that permit the helpee to explore himself and his problem. Responding with empathy at interchangeable levels facilitates client exploration. During this phase of helping, the helper is attempting to get to know the helpee and his or her experience. Confrontations at this stage are least appropriate. Helper responses that go beyond what the helpee has presented are additive in nature and facilitate the second phase of helping, client self-understanding. It is during the understanding phase that confrontations may be introduced, but only when high levels of understanding have been achieved. Confrontation, if it is to be used at all in counseling, is most appropriate in the action phase when a thorough exploration and understanding of the helpee and the problem have been attained. Confrontations have a constructive potential when they are based upon understanding and then applied in the action phase of helping where the helper focuses on the development of constructive behavior change. Premature confrontations are at best an indication of a helper's naivete regarding the helping process and, at worst, an expression of the helper's incompetence.

Berenson and Mitchell (1974) further refine the dimensions of confrontation by identifying the appropriate sequence for the various types of confrontations that occur in the action phase of helping. They view confrontation as a segment of Carkhuff's third phase of helping, the action phase, where other helper initiative and action-oriented dimensions appear. As the different types of confrontations are initiated by the helper, the helpee is guided through a process of exploration, understanding, and action. Experiential confrontations elicit helpee self-exploration because they engage the helpee in a process of experiencing himself/herself as experienced by the helper. Didactic confrontations also serve to facilitate helpee self-exploration as he learns to experience himself in light of new information about himself or his experience. For example, a helper experiential confrontation may be expressed as, "On the one hand you say that alcohol is not a problem for you, yet every time you have trouble in your marriage, drinking is a part of it." Such a confrontation points out the discrepancies presented by the helpee as experienced by the helper. This encourages the helpee to look a little closer at himself and his experience and to explore himself further. An example of a didactic confrontation may be expressed as, "You say you only had two drinks after work last night, yet the breathalyzer test registered a highly intoxicated condition; and your companions report you downed at least a six-pack, and they left while you were still drinking!" Such a confrontation encourages the helpee to look at himself/herself in the light of this information and consider whether or not he/she experienced a blackout or is consciously attempting to con the counselor. In either case, the effect of confrontation is deeper self-exploration.

The experiential and didactic confrontations in the hands of highly responsive helpers are more effective in the initial stage of the action phase. As the helpee explores himself, the helper can effectively utilize a strength or weakness confrontation which sets the stage for helpee self-understanding. Strength and weakness confrontations permit the client to understand himself at new levels. When this occurs, the helpee is ready for action confrontations, as he or she is ready to demonstrate his or her new understanding by specific behavioral change.

The model, then, views confrontation as occurring only when understanding has been established and initiated in the action phase of helping. Within the action phase, the five types of confrontations are more effectively employed in the order of experiential and didactic confrontations to facilitate client self-exploration, strength and weakness confrontations to deepen client self-understanding, and encouragement to action confrontations as a stimulus toward specific behavior change (action). This sequence is presented in Figure 3.

CARKHUFF'S ACTION PHASE:
THE SEQUENCE OF CONFRONTATIONS

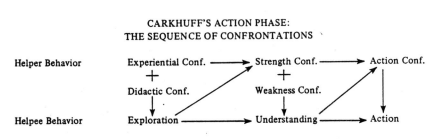

Figure 3. SOURCE: Bernard G. Berenson and Kevin M. Mitchell, *Confrontation for better or worse!* (Amherst, MA: Human Resource Development Press, 1974), p. 86. Reprinted by permission.

The results of recent research on confrontations have unavoidable implications for the counselor committed to effectiveness (summarized in Berenson & Mitchell, 1974). To ignore these implications is to dabble in hit-or-miss helping. In summary, these implications are as follows (Berenson & Mitchell, 1974; Carkhuff, 1969, 1971; Carkhuff & Berenson, 1967):

1. Confrontation can have a constructive or destructive effect on helping. Confrontation can be for better or for worse!
2. Confrontation is never necessary or of itself sufficient. It may, however, be an efficient catalyst to personal growth and development in the hands of a skilled helper.
3. Facilitative confrontation is a set of skills which can be learned.
4. Confrontation is helpful only if it is based upon a deep level of understanding.
5. Only helpers who by their skills demonstrate high levels of understanding have the capability to be facilitative confronters.
6. Confrontation is a helper-initiated skill that must be preceded by helper responsiveness skills if it is to be constructive.

7. Used independently of high levels of empathic understanding, confrontation is negative, hostile, and destructive.
8. Confrontation is most-effective in the action phase of the helping process which is preceded by a thorough process of helpee exploration and understanding.
9. Confrontation can have differential effects upon helping in relation to the types and sequence of confrontations employed.
10. Only those who have the right to help by virtue of their skills have the right to confront.

COUNSELING THE RELUCTANT AND RESISTANT CLIENT

One of the most difficult aspects of alcoholism counseling is working with clients who do not want to be involved in the process or who actively attempt to impede its effectiveness. Counselors are frequently confronted with clients who deny that they have an alcohol problem and who attempt to work against the counselor. The reluctant and resistant client presents a challenge to the counselor that requires an understanding of why it occurs and how it can be dealt with constructively.

Although the difference may be slight, a distinction between client resistance and client reluctance exists. The reluctant client is a person who does not want to be involved in counseling and is only there because he or she has to be. Whether it be through the vehicle of legal intervention, employer ultimatums, or domestic pressure, the client enters counseling with a reluctance that can affect the process significantly. Alcoholism counselors are confronted more frequently with clients who do not want to be involved in counseling than are other helping professionals. It is a rare occurrence for a client to see an alcoholism counselor of his own volition; consequently, knowing how to deal with such clients is an important issue for counselors.

The resistant client also sets the stage for blocking counselor effectiveness, although there is a distinction from the reluctant client. Resistance involves client attitudes and behaviors that fight the treatment process. This can involve both overt and hidden processes evidenced by clients who want to be in counseling as well as those who do not. The expression of a client's resistance may be direct or symbolic in nature and may thus require a greater degree of clinical understanding than the concept of reluctance. As both of these issues are common to alcoholism counseling, they will be dealt with in terms of gaining an understanding of them as significant treatment issues. Specific strategies the counselor can use when confronted with these issues will also be presented.

Having to work with reluctant clients seems to be the rule rather than the exception in alcoholism counseling. Most alcoholic clients do not enter counseling voluntarily and do not want to be there. At the onset of counseling, such clients reject the counselors and begin looking for ways to keep the counselor from being effective. How the client became involved in counseling will affect the nature and scope of the reluctance. If a referral had come from the courts, for example, the reluctance is likely to be different than if the referral had come from another human service provider. A client who must attend counseling in order to keep his/her license is likely to displace hostility onto the counselor. Another example of a reluctant client is the person who is forced into treatment in order to preserve his or her job. In such situations, clients often give lip service to counseling but let it be known that they do not want to be involved in treatment.

The key variable in working with reluctant clients is the counselor's reaction. It is natural for clients who are forced into treatment to be cautious and hesitant about counseling, but this does not have to be necessarily negative. If the counselor is skilled enough to recognize a client's reluctance, understand it, and respond to it facilitatively, the results can be highly therapeutic. For example, a client may express his or her reluctance through anger and hostility or by being silent and withdrawn during counseling. An ineffective counselor will respond to the initial behavioral set of the client, but the more effective helper will respond to what is beneath this overt behavior. A client's response to counseling may be "It wasn't my idea to come here. I'm here because I have to be in order to keep my job. So what are you going to do for me?" On the surface, the client's reluctance is expressed as hostility, but beneath this may be fear and/or a sense of hopelessness. When working with reluctant clients, counselors need to be careful of becoming defensive or of trying to win over the client by apologizing for the client's predicament. Clients are only "won over" by the effectiveness a counselor demonstrates in his/her ability to respond to the client in a manner that goes beyond what is superficially presented. A counselor's response to the above statement from a reluctant client might be, "It angers you to be here. But it also sounds like you're frightened because you're not sure whether or not I've got something to offer you." Such a response attends to what the client gave the counselor but also goes beyond it in such a manner that further exploration is encouraged. It also lets the client know the counselor has control of the situation and that he or she warrants the client's confidence.

Clients may present themselves reluctantly because they are not sure of what to expect from counseling. They may be receiving enough secondary gains from their condition that they fear counseling may take away the benefits they receive. For some, sobriety can mean added responsibility which they prefer to avoid. Client reluctance may also be defensive behavior that serves to protect the client's self-esteem. In such situations, the need for counseling may be equated with failure.

Dealing with the reluctant client is a test of the counselor's skill. Frequently the reluctant client who does not cooperate causes the counselor to react in a variety of nonproductive ways. Ineffective counselors tend to feed into the client's reluctance by trying too hard to do well. It is almost as if the counselor accepts responsibility for the client's reluctance and blames himself for the lack of progress. An over-investment in succeeding rather than understanding what is going on beyond the behavioral manifestations the client portrays causes counselors to lose control of the relationship and become engulfed in client manipulations. Such attempts to win clients over only serve to add to the problem. Counselors should avoid getting into psychological wrestling matches over a client's reluctance to be involved in counseling. A better alternative is to accept the reluctance as a reality related to external events and to not get bogged down by it or take it personally. A counselor response such as "You're really uptight because you don't want to be here. It is as if you're trapped and no one gives a damn. As long as you have to be here, let's explore the ways that we can make this experience a freeing one for you," lets the client know that the counselor accepts the reluctance, understands it, but will not be engulfed by it. The important thing is to accept a client's reluctant feelings and to deal with them in the context of getting beyond them. A client's reluctance is a reflection of the person, and thus it must first be understood before any further progress can be made in counseling (Kennedy, 1977).

Client resistance to counseling is usually more subtle than client reluctance and is related more to the intrapersonal dynamics of the individual. Whereas the reluctant client is consciously aware that he or she does not want to be involved in counseling, resistance can be both conscious and unconscious. A resistant client more often than not is resisting the idea of getting well rather than directly resisting the counselor. Many alcoholic clients resist counseling because of the anxiety generated by the implications of abstinence. They do not want to give up "benefits" of their illness, such as attention they receive, escape from responsibility, or avoidance of painful situations. Sobriety may mean having to face situations they had previously been avoiding. At a deeper intrapsychic level, some alcoholic clients may resist counseling because of an unconscious desire to inflict harm upon themselves. Continued drinking in such cases fulfills the pathological need to punish oneself which often stems from unresolved guilt. Thus, to understand the place of resistance in counseling, counselors need to view it in light of the client's overall personality structure as opposed to a specific behavioral incident.

Resistance may be expressed in several ways. One of the most common ways it is manifested is through silence. Silence is sometimes a difficult thing for counselors to handle as it can create significant performance anxiety. There is a tendency for counselors to become anxious with prolonged silence and ask questions of the client as a means of breaking through this resistance. It is usually best to listen to the client's silence rather than to try and break it, as many cues are given by nonverbal gestures and behavior. By listening to a client's silence, data is obtained from which an open-ended response can be made by the counselor. Asking questions that require simply a yes or no answer, or attacking the silence, rewards the client for being resistant and may deepen rather than resolve the silence (Kennedy, 1977).

On the other extreme, resistance may be expressed by a monopolizing talkativeness on the client's part. In these situations, clients attempt to keep a safe distance from those areas that are emotionally difficult to deal with by diverting a counselor's attention. Changing topics, talking hysterically, or shifting emphasis are verbal manipulations clients often use to resist the efforts of the counselor to discuss sensitive areas. It is best for counselors in such situations to direct a response that calls attention to what the client is doing without being derogatory to the client as a person. For example, the counselor may say, "It really is hard to focus on specific concerns this way. You seem torn between wanting to talk about significant material and talking about irrelevancies."

Another form of resistance is apparent when clients keep the counselor from getting close by intellectualizing. Intellectualization is a defense whereby clients objectify their problems and emotionally distance themselves from their concerns. It is a difficult resistance to deal with because clients talk about their problems in great clarity but their feelings are not involved. In dealing with intellectualizing clients, counselors need to remember that the defense is primarily unconcious in nature, and therefore great skill is required to deal with it so as not to reinforce it. Often counselors revert to intellectualizing themselves in response to the client, which results in a verbal tennis match where both parties lose. It is best to understand why clients are intellectualizing and respond to the emotional material that is being protected by the verbal defenses of the clients.

Another form of resistance in counseling occurs when clients are vague and general in relation to their own emotions. By generalizing their feelings, they continue to protect their inner selves. In such cases, the client keeps his/her emotions at a safe distance by not linking them to any specific person or subject. He or she tends to talk in vague generalizations and abstractions without being concrete or specific. This is particularly true of clients who have had a long history of alcoholism. Their drinking has caused them to lose touch with themselves, and they often have great difficulty in relating to their emotions again. Counselors need to understand that generalizations are an unintentional form of resistance. In most cases, the client has difficulty relating specifically to his emotions because he has forgotten how to do so. The role of the counselor is to model and to teach the client how to explore anew his emotional responses to people and events.

When clients are superficially happy, continually laughing, or making light of things, they may actually be resisting the counselor. This is a resistance tactic to which insecure counselors who feel they need a client's approval are particularly vulnerable. Such clients stay on the surface by joking, lightly dismissing material that may be of significant value, and avoiding discussion of anything that may have a painful aspect. Clients who continually report that everything is fine are usually afraid of getting into meaningful material because it may mean experiencing pain. Sometimes counselors become impatient with such clients and confront them inappropriately. It is important to understand that a person who is expending so much energy to make things appear fine usually has a lot of anxiety about facing things directly. A direct confrontation without meaningful understanding will only reinforce the client's fear. Counselors need to understand what lies behind this carefree, assured defense and explore this material in a manner that enables the client to let go of his defenses.

There are other indirect resistances that clients may not be aware of which should be dealt with in counseling. Such behaviors as switching appointments, frequently coming late, coming to sessions intoxicated, making excuses, or not paying therapy bills can be forms of indirect resistance. It is as if the client is attempting all kinds of behavior to keep the counselor distracted and off guard. Such clients enter into a nonverbal one-upmanship contract to see how far the counselor can be manipulated. These testing-out behaviors serve to resist the counselor's effort to get close to the client. When counselors react with impatience or inappropriate confrontations, it serves to confirm the client's impression that the counselor is no different from other people he or she has learned to successfully manipulate. While such client behavior needs to be confronted, understanding must precede the confrontation if it is going to free the client to get beyond his/her defenses.

A final resistance to be considered is a client's seductive behavior. This is usually so subtle in nature that it frequently goes unnoticed, particularly by inexperienced counselors. The effect of seductive behavior, like all resistance strategies, is to slow down counseling progress and thereby avoid dealing with emotionally significant material. Seductiveness may be sexual in nature or it may take the form of flattery, gifts, compliments, and other verbal or nonverbal behaviors. While such behavior is a means of gaining attention or approval, it is also a way of gaining control of the relationship. When a counselor responds defensively or succumbs to the seductiveness, the goal of distracting the counselor has been achieved and the client knows he/she is safe. Seductive clients can be difficult to deal with if the counselor is unaware of what is stimulating this behavior. As in all forms of resistance, the counselor needs to avoid getting caught up in the specific behavior and should work to understand what the client is really attempting to say. Making reference to specific resistant behaviors should be used only as a tool to further explore the nature of the resistance so that clients can attain a deeper understanding of themselves and their relationship to their world.

Counseling reluctant and resistant clients is an integral part of alcoholism counseling. The reasons for a client's reluctance to be involved in counseling need to be thoroughly explored and understood if counselors are to avoid getting sidetracked. Likewise, client resistance should be viewed as a manipulative defense of troubled people. Resistance needs to be understood for what it is saying about the person and not attacked because it may be frustrating to the counselor. Understanding and working through resistance may give the needed impetus toward a deeper and more effective therapeutic relationship.

TERMINATION IN COUNSELING

Termination is one of the most important therapeutic processes in counseling. Many counseling relationships fail to make a significant impact because good termination procedures were either ignored, avoided, or just forgotten. Adequate closure of counseling sessions and counseling relationships is essential in order to provide feedback to clients by reviewing the progress that was made, reinforcing the continuance of positive changes, and signifying that a new beginning for the client is about to commence. Termination is a significant treatment issue for alcoholism counselors which often accounts for the difference between successful and unsuccessful therapeutic interventions. This section will explore some of the more prevalent issues involved in effective and ineffective termination and suggest some specific guidelines for appropriate termination procedures.

While there are a variety of theoretical viewpoints regarding the role of termination in counseling, there is a general consensus that termination is a process signifying the beginning of growth rather than the end of a relationship. It is a commencement, not a dissolution (Johnson & Vestermark, 1970; Mueller & Kell, 1966; Yalom, 1970).

Reasons for Termination

Termination can be initiated by either the counselor or the client for several different reasons. When counseling has been successful, termination is initiated because it is recognized that the goals of the helping relationship have been achieved and the time has come for the client to be on his/her own. Even with the knowledge that termination is imminent, the loss of a meaningful relationship can be difficult for both the counselor and the client. As is the case in any meaningful relationship in which one has a vested interest, there is a sense of loss upon termination. It is important for counselors to deal openly with their feelings and to communicate these to the client, as it serves to model the integration of one's emotions and behavior. It also communicates an acceptance of one's emotions as well as the recognition that growth means risking loss. When the counselor shares his/her feelings honestly, it is easier for the client to in turn share his/her own feelings and take the necessary steps toward a new beginning. This is particularly crucial for the alcoholic, who must process loss constructively as part of his recovery.

In a successful counseling experience, it is common for the client to be hesitant about terminating. The anxiety of having to face life without the help of the counselor can be difficult for the client. A counselor may attempt to initiate termination but find the client constantly avoiding the issue. It is important for the counselor to explore whether this is a result of a natural anxiety about being on one's own or whether it is an indication of an unhealthy dependency upon the counselor. Talking about the feasibility of termination can serve as a barometer to measure client dependency as well as his/her readiness to terminate. If termination is appropriate, the client would have moved from dependency upon the counselor to behavioral indications that he or she can now trust his/her own feelings, attitudes, and behavior without the approval or input of the counselor. The client's movement from initial dependency to self-reliance and independence is an indicator that counseling has been successful and discussion of termination is appropriate.

Although it may be emotionally difficult for the client and the counselor to terminate when counseling has been successful, there is a joy, a sense of accomplishment, and satisfaction that something constructive has taken place. When counseling has not been successful, termination can be an awkward and painful experience for both the counselor and the client. A counselor may no longer feel capable of working with the client because of a lack of knowledge, experience, or skill

(Korchin, 1976). Perhaps the counselor realizes that he has lost his objectivity, or he recognizes that an impasse has been reached. In such situations, he or she sees that the experience, for whatever reason, is not a successful one and that, in the client's best interest, counseling must be terminated. While in most cases counselors should have the necessary discipline to work through these issues with clients, many cannot, and thus termination is the only responsible alternative. It is extremely important that the counselor in such situations clarifies the reasons for termination to alleviate any possible sense of guilt that clients may assume. Part of effective termination in such cases involves helping the client find another counselor, if appropriate, and making sure that the reasons for termination are clearly understood (Korchin, 1976). When counseling is terminated by the counselor because he judges it to be unproductive, the client's feelings must be dealt with openly, honestly, and sensitively.

The client may recognize that counseling is not helping, become dissatisfied, and consequently terminate. There may be valid reasons for the client's dissatisfaction, and these should be thoroughly explored. However, the client's expression of dissatisfaction may be a defense against the anxiety of dealing with change. It is a common experience in alcoholism counseling for clients to express hostility towards being involved in counseling and to terminate on this basis. Client attempts to terminate may also be manipulative acts through which they try to gain control of the relationship by threatening to abandon it. The naive counselor can get trapped in such situations and his/her potency as a helper will consequently be diminished. The skilled counselor will recognize that in such cases the issue of termination is a camouflage, and he or she will then facilitatively confront the client.

Clients may be dissatisfied with counseling and wish to terminate because they do not like the counselor. Sometimes it is best to curtail further involvement if interpersonal difficulties exist. Counselors need to be careful to not always be looking for the deep psychological reasons to explain client dislike, but to briefly explore it and accept it for what it is. In such situations, counselors should attempt to help the client find a counselor with whom he or she may find compatibility. The appropriate matching of counselors with clients is an area that is receiving increasing attention in the research literature as a variable that can alter the process and results of counseling (Lasky, 1974; Mendelsohn & Geller, 1965; Sapolsky, 1970).

Resistance to Termination

Because termination entails emotional intensity, it can be resisted by both the counselor and the client. The counselor may have a tendency to avoid terminating because he or she does not want to let go of a meaningful relationship. The counselor may have lost perspective and find the relationship meeting his own needs and unnecessarily prolong counseling. He may also find that he needs the client for his own professional esteem and will thus resist terminating when it is actually the best alternative for the client. Counselors may have difficulty themselves in coming to terms with the emotions involved in loss and avoid the process of termination. Such resistances often surface in the form of superficial, premature, and/or incomplete termination.

Clients often resist termination for several reasons. For some, counseling has become a way of life representing their only source of emotional support, and the thought of losing it can be overwhelming. While it is natural to have some anxiety concerning severance of such an important relationship, emotional over-reaction to termination is a sign that the client may not be prepared to make it on his/her own. A client may also view the idea of termination as a rejection, even though termination, when handled appropriately, is in actuality an affirmation of self. Clients may experience a reoccurrence of the symptoms that brought them to a counselor, or they may experience generalized distress and anxiety. It is important for counselors to recognize that these reactions are normal. Counselors should deal with these reactions as part of the termination process so that clients view them as normal also. The danger in not handling these issues appropriately is that the clients' dependency, rather than their autonomy, may be what is reinforced.

Premature Termination

Counseling is often terminated prematurely for reasons that are beyond the counselor's control. External events such as illness, employment change, vacation, or administrative dictates can place the counselor in the uncomfortable position of knowing that he or she must terminate with his/her clients even though it is not the appropriate time. Although the reasons for premature termination may be beyond anyone's control, there are still likely to generate strong client feelings that need to be discussed openly. If a good therapeutic relationship has been established, the client may feel betrayed by early termination. The client who entered counseling with an intent to explore himself/herself and to learn how to change may feel resentment and intense anger towards the counselor. In the client's view, the counselor has not lived up to his end of the contract. There may be anxiety on the client's part that some of the sensitive things talked about in therapy may be shared with someone else, especially when the client is transferred to another counselor. The client may feel abandoned because the one to whom he opened and the one he thought could "put him back together again" is leaving. The client may also blame himself for the premature termination and feel guilty about it. He or she may see this as just another rejection confirming a negative self-image, or there may be strong hurt and pain in reaction to the loss of a meaningful relationship.

Premature termination resulting from external events is likely to generate intense emotional reactions for the client (Eisenberg & Delaney, 1977). While this may cause some discomfort for the counselor that can influence him or her to avoid discussing the client's feelings, it is crucial that these feelings be dealt with thoroughly, openly, and in a nondefensive and nonevaluative manner. It is appropriate for the counselor to share his/her own feelings as well. For example, the counselor may say, "I'm very upset about this also and I did not expect it to happen. It makes me feel hurt that I have to end counseling in this way."' By being honest with the client, the counselor models appropriate self-disclosure and encourages emotional expression. This will help pave the way for a discussion of what has been accomplished to date in the counseling process and for preparation for the next steps, whether they be transferring to another counselor or going on independently. The important thing is to thoroughly process and not avoid the emotions surrounding a premature termination. Even though premature termination due to external events may be cause for discomfort, it can result in productive and growth-producing termination if handled appropriately.

Premature termination may occur for other reasons. A counselor's confrontation or encouragement of the client to act in certain ways may result in the client terminating counseling. Often an effective counselor is terminated by the client because the client realizes he or she cannot manipulate the counselor. In such situations, clients will terminate and find a counselor who will provide safety and security without the threat of change. It is as if the counselor and client enter into a destructive pact of "I won't expose your ineptitude as a helper if you won't make me face my weakness as a person." Such alliances are destructive and pathological for both the counselor and the client.

A client may prematurely terminate counseling and reject the counselor because he or she does not view counseling as beneficial. There may be a valid or invalid base for such feelings which should be explored by the counselor. When a counselor is rejected by the client, it is important that he or she be aware of the emotional reactions resulting from this rejection. It is natural for the counselor to feel hurt and angry when rejected. Counselors are human! But it is also important for the counselor to process these feelings and not think that he is beyond them. Processing rather than avoiding or denying these feelings is more likely to have favorable consequences for the counselor. How the counselor responds to premature client-initiated termination can make the difference between a constructive or ineffectual experience for the client.

Specific Techniques for Termination

Effectively terminating individual sessions is an important aspect in preparing clients for the final termination of a counseling relationship. Bramer and Shostrum (1968) suggest several techniques that can be used by a counselor in initiating the termination of individual sessions as well as of cases. Reference to time limits is one way to remind the client that the session is about to end. It is best for the counselor to inform the client of time limits at the beginning of the session so that closure is not abrupt. Summarizing is a second suggestion (Bramer and Shostrum, 1968) for terminating a session. A counselor's summarizing of the essential factors of the session or asking the client to summarize what he or she perceives has occurred is a helpful means of closing a session. Reference to the future is a third suggestion where the counselor can gracefully indicate the end of the particular session while also communicating his/her intent to continue. "Our time is about up for today. When would you like to meet next week?" cues the client to the end but also looks to continuing the relationship. Tapering off in intensity is another suggestion for terminating a session. The counselor should attempt to reduce intensity as the session comes to a close so that the client does not leave in a state of emotional upheaval.

Bramer and Shostrum (1968) also make some helpful suggestions for terminating cases. Verbal preparation statements, such as "This is our last session and you certainly have accomplished a lot. How do you see yourself carrying on from here?", is one way to signal an end as well as to explore the client's preparation for the future. Another example may be for the counselor to say, "You seem to be at a point where you can work things out for yourself. Let's discuss some of your thoughts on how you plan to go on from here." Bramer and Shostrum also suggest that counselors work out a final summary statement that reviews the accomplishments of counseling and establishes goals and action steps to be taken in the future. If a referral is to be made, then termination would involve structuring a smooth transition to the new counselor. The formal ending of a case should always be warm and encouraging, with the counselor expressing confidence in the client's ability to continue the growth started in counseling. It should also be clear that the counselor is available in the future if he or she should be needed and that it would be good to hear from the client. This reinforces the counselor's genuine concern for the client and keeps the door open for further involvement if necessary.

General Guidelines for Effective Termination

Understanding the important role of termination in the counseling process is the first step toward developing terminating skills. Without effective termination skills, effective helping will not be realized. Potentially effective helpers minimize their impact by neglecting this crucial aspect of the counseling process. Termination issues represent a dynamic process that is constantly operable in counseling. There are elements of termination in every counseling session, and there is also a termination that is cumulative and final in nature.

For effective termination to occur, it is important that it be viewed as a beginning and not as an end. While termination does mean a change, the change is a positive one that will facilitate a new start. This perspective is best understood when termination procedures are linked to the goals that were established when therapy began (Zaro et al., 1977). Termination, properly implemented, is indicative of accomplishment. It should always begin by a review of the reasons why the client first came to counseling and by an honest evaluation of whether or not these have now been sufficiently attended to. If termination is linked to the goals the client has made, it will facilitate his or her perception of termination as an accomplishment and not as an indication of failure. One of the goals of helping is to assist people in becoming more self-reliant, independent, autonomous, and better able to act constructively in their world. With such a perspective, termination is a process that signifies accomplishment.

The initiation of termination procedures should not be

abrupt. It generally takes several sessions to terminate as there
are likely to be several emotional reactions to work through
before the final terminating session. Counselors need to be
ready to adapt according to the client's needs, as initiating
termination may serve to signal that there is much more to
accomplish in therapy and that termination should be held in
suspension. When termination is initiated by either the counselor or the client, it is important for the counselor to be aware
of the feelings surrounding this issue and be prepared to deal
with them. There is likely to be a variety of ambivalent feelings
about termination which should be processed.

In addition to these general considerations which present a
perspective for counselors to view termination, there are specific guidelines to be considered, as follows:

1. Termination is an integral part of the counseling process
   and should be attended to in the initial sessions.
2. The goals of the counseling relationship should serve as a
   criteria for determining when termination is inappropriate.
3. The counselor should encourage the client's expression of
   feelings about terminating and also be willing to share
   his/her own feelings.
4. Termination is an opportunity to provide constructive
   feedback for the client and to integrate the learning acquired in counseling with a direction for the future.
5. Termination is an opportunity for the client to experience
   fully how personal growth never stops. Termination represents a transition to new phases of growth.
6. Termination should review accomplishments, emphasize
   the strengths of the client, be encouraging, and leave open
   the option to return and review one's progress.
7. In working with groups, termination should be an open
   process with members discussing the issue and providing
   feedback to members who wish to terminate.
8. When there is mutual agreement that counseling has
   served its function, termination is appropriate.

EPILOGUE

ALCOHOLISM counseling is a profession with a mission. Its mission is to provide healing to those suffering from the illness of alcoholism and renewal to loved ones affected by this disease. The fulfillment of this mission is dependent upon the alcoholism counselor's dedication, skill, and, most of all, his or her ability to love.

This book has attempted to contribute to the building of the profession of alcoholism counseling. Perspectives on the issues discussed in this book have been presented to stimulate, provoke, and encourage alcoholism counselors to become involved in shaping the future course of this profession.

BIBLIOGRAPHY

Abroms, G.M. Supervision as metatherapy. In F. Kaslow & Associates: *Supervision, Consultation, and Staff Training in the Helping Professions.* San Francisco: Jossey-Bass, 1977.

Ajzen, R. Human values and counseling. *The Personnel and Guidance Journal, 52(2)*:77-81, 1973.

Altucher, N. Constructive use of the supervisory relationship. *Journal of Counseling Psychology, 14*:165-170, 1967.

American Personnel and Guidance Association. *Position Statement on Counselor Licensure.* Washington, D.C., 1975.

Anthony, W.A. *Principles of Psychiatric Rehabilitation.* Amherst, Mass.: HRD Press, 1978.

Anthony, W.A. & Carkhuff, R.R. *The Art of Health Care.* Amherst, Mass.: HRD Press, 1976.

Anthony, W.A., Dell Orto, A., Lasky, R., Marinelli, R., Power, P., & Spaniol, L. A training model for rehabilitation counselor education. *Rehabilitation Counseling Bulletin*, March, 1977.

Arbuckle, D.S. Supervision: Learning, not counseling. *Journal of Counseling Psychology, 12*:90-94, 1965.

Arbuckle, D.S. Counselor licensure: To be or not to be. *The Personnel and Guidance Journal, 55*:581-585, 1977.

Archer, J. & Kagan, N. Teaching interpersonal relationship skills on campus: A pyramid approach. *Journal of Counseling Psychology, 20*:535-540, 1973.

Barclay, J.R. *Counseling and Philosophy: A Theoretical Exposition.* Guidance Monograph Series. Boston: Houghton-Mifflin, 1968.

Bellucci, J.E. Microcounseling and imitation learning: A behavioral approach to counselor education. *Counselor Education and Supervision, 12*:88-97, 1972.

Benjamin, A. *The Helping Interview.* Boston: Houghton-Mifflin, 1974.

Berenson, B.G. & Mitchell, K. *Confrontation: For Better or Worse.* Amherst, Mass.: HRD Press, 1974.

Berenson, D.H. The effects of systematic human relations training upon the classroom performance of elementary school teachers. *Journal of Research and Development in Education, 4*:70-85, 1971.

Blocher, D.H. *Developmental Counseling.* New York: Ronald Press, 1966.

Bower, S. & Bower, G. *Asserting Yourself.* Reading, Mass.; Addison-Wesley, 1976.

Boyd, J.D. Microcounseling for a counseling-like verbal response set:

Differential effects of two micromodels and two methods of counseling supervision. *Journal of Counseling Psychology, 20*:97-98, 1973.

Boyd, J.D. *Counselor Supervision.* Muncie, Ind.: Accelerated Development, Inc., 1978.

Bramer, L. & Shostrum, C. *Therapeutic Psychology.* Englewood Cliffs, N.J.: Prentice-Hall, 1968.

Brown, W.T. Effectiveness of paraprofessionals: The evidence. *Personnel and Guidance Journal, 53*:257-263, 1974.

Carkhuff, R.R. *Helping and Human Relationships: A Primer for Lay and Professional Helpers.* vols. 1 & 2. New York: Holt, Rinehart & Winston, 1969.

Carkhuff, R.R. *The Development of Human Resources: Education, Psychology, and Social Change.* New York: Holt, Rinehart & Winston, 1971.

Carkhuff, R.R. New directions in training for the helping professions: Toward a technology for human and community resource development. *The Counseling Psychologist, 3(3)*:12-30, 1972.

Carkhuff, R.R. *Cry twice! From Custody to Treatment: The Story of Institutional Change.* Amherst, Mass.: HRD Press, 1974.

Carkhuff, R.R. & Berenson, B.G. *Beyond Counseling and Therapy,* 1st ed. New York: Holt, Rinehart & Winston, 1967.

Carkhuff, R.R. & Berenson, B.G. *Teaching as Treatment.* Amherst, Mass.: HRD Press, 1976.

Carkhuff, R.R. & Berenson, B.G. *Beyond Counseling and Therapy,* 2nd ed. New York: Holt, Rinehart & Winston, 1977.

Carkhuff, R.R. & Pierce, R. *The Art of Helping.* Amherst, Mass.: HRD Press, 1975.

Carkhuff, R.R. & Truax, C.B. Lay mental health counseling: The effects of lay group counseling. *Journal of Consulting Psychology, 29*:426-431, 1965.

Carkhuff, R.R. & Truax, C.B. Training in counseling and psychotherapy: An evaluation of an integrated didactic and experimental approach. *Journal of Consulting Psychology, 29*:333-336, 1965.

Clinebell, H. *Understanding and Counseling the Alcoholic.* Nashville, Tenn.: Abingdon Press, 1968.

Daubner, E.V. & Daubner, E.S. Ethics and counseling decisions. *The Personnel and Guidance Journal, 48(6)*:434-442, 1970.

Delworth, et al. *Student Paraprofessionals: A Working Model for Higher Education.* APGA Student Personnel Series Monograph No. 17, Washington, D.C.: APGA, 1974.

Dendy, R.F. A model for the training of undergraduate residence hall assistants as paraprofessional counselors using videotape playback techniques and interpersonal process recall. Ph.D. dissertation, Michigan State University, 1971.

Dyer, W. *Modern Theory and Method in Group Training.* New York: Van Nostrand Reinhold, 1972.

Eastern Area Alcohol Education and Training Program. *A Manual of Accreditation Standards for Alcoholism Counselor Training Programs.* Bloomfield, Conn., 1977.

Eisenberg, S. & Delaney, D.J. Using video stimulation of counseling for training counselors. *Journal of Counseling Psychology, 17:*15-19, 1970.

Eisenberg, S. & Delaney, D.J. *The Counseling Process.* Chicago, Illinois: Rand McNally, 1977.

Ellis, A. *Humanistic Psychotherapy. The Rational-Emotive Approach.* New York: Julian Press, 1973.

Forster, J. What shall we do about credentialing? *The Personnel and Guidance Journal, 55:*573-576, 1977.

Freleigh, P.W. & Buchheimer, A. The use of peer groups in practicum supervision. *Counselor Education and Supervision, 8:*284-288, 1969.

Gartner, A. & Riessman, R. Changing the professions: The new careers strategy. In R. Gross & P. Osterman (Eds.): *The New Professionals.* New York: Simon & Schuster, 1972.

Gartner, A. & Riessman, R. The paraprofessional movement in perspective. *The Personnel and Guidance Journal, 54(4):*253-256, 1974.

Goldstein, A.P. *Psychotherapeutic Attraction.* Elmsford, N.Y.: Pergamon, 1971.

Gross, S. Professional disclosure: An alternative to licensing. *The Personnel and Guidance Journal, 55:*586-588, 1977.

Guy, E. *Synanon.* New York: Doubleday & Co., 1968.

Hefele, T.J. The effects of systematic human relations training upon student achievement. *Journal of Research and Development in Education, 4:*52-69, 1971.

Hoffman, A.M. Paraprofessional effectiveness. *Personnel and Guidance Journal, 54:*494-497, 1976.

Howard, D. & Howard, N. *Family Approach to Problem Drinking.* Columbia, Mo.: Family Training Center, 1976.

Hughes, E. Professions. *Daedalus, 92* (Fall, 1963):655-668.

Hultman, K. Values as defenses. *The Personnel and Guidance Journal, 54:*269-271, 1976.

Ivey, A.E. *Microcounseling.* Springfield: Thomas, 1971.

Johnson, D.E. & Vestermark, M.J. *Barriers and Hazards in Counseling.* Boston: Houghton-Mifflin, 1970.

Johnson, V.E. *I'll Quit Tomorrow.* New York: Harper & Row, 1973.

Kadushin, A. *Supervision in Social Work.* New York: Columbia Univ. Press, 1976.

Kagan, N. & Krathwohl, D.R. *Studies in Human Interaction: Interpersonal Process Recall Stimulated by Videotape.* East Lansing, Mich.: Educational Publishing Services, 1967.

Kagan, N., Krathwohl, D.R., & Miller, R. Stimulated recall in therapy using videotape: A case study. *Journal of Counseling Psychology, 10*:237-243, 1963.

Kagan, N. & Schauble, F.G. Affect simulation in interpersonal process recall. *Journal of Counseling Psychology, 16*:309-313, 1969.

Kaslow, F. & Associates. *Supervision, Consultation, and Staff Training in the Helping Professions.* San Francisco: Jossey-Bass, 1977.

Kell, B.L. & Mueller, W.J. *Impact and Change: A Study of Counseling Relationships.* New York: Appleton-Century-Crofts, P.H. 1966.

Kemp, C.G. *Intangibles in Counseling.* Boston: Houghton-Mifflin, 1967.

Kennedy, E. *On Becoming a Counselor.* New York: Seabury Press, 1977.

Korchin, S.J. *Modern Clinical Psychology: Principles of Intervention in the Clinic and Community.* New York: Basic Books, 1976.

Kutzik, A. The medical field. In F. Kaslow & Associates: *Supervision, Consultation, and Staff Training in the Helping Professions.* San Francisco: Jossey-Bass, 1977.

Lasky, R. *The Influence of Counselor Status and Counselor-Client Congruency on Interpersonal Attractions in the Counseling Interview.* Paper presented at APGA National Convention, New Orleans, Louisiana, 1974.

Lazarus, A. *Behavior Therapy and Beyond.* New York: McGraw-Hill, 1971.

Lazarus, A. Women in behavior therapy. In V. Franks & L. Burthe (Eds.): *Women in Therapy: New Psychotherapies for a Changing Society.* New York: Brunn/Mazel, 1974.

Mann, J.H. & Mann, C.H. The effect of role-playing experience on role-playing ability. In B.J. Biddle & E.J. Thomas (Eds.): *Role-Theory: Concepts and Research.* New York: John Wiley & Sons, 1966.

Marcus, G. How casework training may be adapted to meet workers personal problems. In *Proceedings of the National Conference of Social Work.* Chicago: Univ. of Chicago Press, 1927.

Maslach, C. Burned-out. *Human Behavior, 519*(September):16-22, 1976.

Mass. Dept. of Public Health. *Confidentiality Manual.* MDPH, Division of Alcoholism, 1976.

McGowan, J.F. & Schmidt, L.D. *Counseling: Readings in Theory and Practice.* New York: Holt, Rinehart & Winston, 1962.

Mendelsohn, G.A. & Geller, M.H. Structure of client attitudes toward counseling and their relation to client-counselor similarity. *Journal of Consulting Psychology, 29*:63-72, 1965.

Moore, W. *The Professions: Role and Rules.* New York: Russell Sage Foundation, 1970.

Muchowski, P. & Valle, S.K. Effects of assertive training on trainers and their spouses. *Journal of Marriage and Family Counseling,* July 1977, pp. 57-62.

Mueller, W. & Kell, B. *Impact and Change.* New York: Appleton-Century-Crofts, P.H., 1966.

Mueller, W. & Kell, B. *Coping with Conflict*. New York: Appleton-Century-Crofts, P.H., 1972.

National Association of Social Workers: *Standards for social service manpower*. New York, 1973.

National Institute on Alcohol Abuse and Alcoholism. *Final report of the ADAMHA/NIAAA planning panel on alcoholism counselor credentialing*, February 1977.

Patterson, C.H. Supervising students in the counseling practicum. *Journal of Counseling Psychology*, *11*:47-53, 1964.

Phillips, D. & Older, H. A model for counseling troubled supervisors. *Alcohol Health and Research World*, 2:24-30, 1977.

Pietrofessa, J.J. & Vriend, J. *The School Counselor as a Professional*. Itasca, Ill.: Peacock, 1971.

Powell, D. *Manpower Needs in the Alcohol Field*. Bloomfield, Conn.: Eastern Area Alcohol Education and Training Program, 1976.

Raths, L.E., Harmin, M., & Simon, S.B. *Values in Teaching*. Columbus, Ohio: Charles E. Merrill, 1966.

Roemer, R. Trends in licensure, certification, and accreditation. *Journal of Allied Health*, *3(1)*:26-33, 1974.

Rogers, C.R. The necessary and sufficient conditions for therapeutic personality change. *Journal of Consulting Psychologists*, *21*:95-101, 1957.

Rogers, C.R. The interpersonal relationship: The core of guidance. *Harvard Educational Review*, *32* (Fall): 416-429, 1962.

Rogers, C.R. Some new challenges. *American Psychologist*, *28*:379-387, 1973.

Rokeach, M. *Beliefs, Attitudes, and Values*. San Francisco: Jossey-Bass, 1970.

Rosenberg, C.M. Making training work. *Proceedings, 4th Annual Alcoholism Conference*. NIAAA, 1975, pp. 406-418.

Rosenberg, C.M., Gerrein, J.R., Manohar, V., & Liftik, J. Evaluation of training of alcoholism counselors. *Journal of Studies on Alcohol*, *37(9)*:1236-1246, 1976.

Sapolsky, A. Relationship between patient-doctor compatibility, mutual perception, and outcome of treatment. *Journal of Abnormal Psychology*, *17*:115-118, 1970.

Scheibe, K.E. *Beliefs and Values*. New York: Holt, Rinehart & Winston, 1970.

Shimberg, B., Esser, B.F., & Kruger, D.H. *Occupational Licensing and Public Policy*. Princeton, N.J.: Educational Testing Service, 1972.

Simon, S.B., Howe, C.W., & Kirschenbaum, H. *Values Clarification*. New York: Hart, 1972.

Solomone, P. Professionalism and unionism in rehabilitation counseling. *Rehabilitation Counseling Bulletin*, *15(3)*:137-146, 1972.

Spivack, J.D. The use of developmental tasks for training counselors using interpersonal process recall. Ph.D. dissertation, Michigan State University, 1970.

Staub, G. & Kent, L. (Eds.): *The Para-professional in the Treatment of*

Alcoholism. Springfield: Thomas, 1973.

Stefflre, B. (Ed.): *Theories of Counseling*. New York: McGraw-Hill, 1965.

Sue, D. Consumerism in counseling. Editorial. *The Personnel and Guidance Journal*, December 1977.

Sweeney, T. & Witmer, J. Who says you're a counselor? *The Personnel and Guidance Journal*, 55:589-594, 1977.

Thursz, D. *Consumer Involvement in Rehabilitation*. Washington, D.C.: U.S. Department of Health, Education, and Welfare, Social and Rehabilitation Service, 1969.

Truax, C. & Lister, J. Effectiveness of counselors and counselor aides. *Journal of Counseling Psychology*, 17(4):331-334, 1970.

U.S. Department of Health, Education, and Welfare. *Credentialing Health Manpower*. Public Health Service, July 1977.

Valle, S.K. Consumer involvement in community alcoholism programs: The Taunton Model. *Alcohol Health and Research World*, Winter, 1975/1976.

Valle, S.K. The effects of training alcoholism workers in human relations, problem solving and program development skills as compared to traditional training methods (Doctoral dissertation, Boston University, Boston, Mass.). *Dissertation Abstracts International*, 36:7313-A-7314-A, 1976.

Valle, S.K. The relative effectiveness of degreed and non-degreed alcoholism counselors. *Maryland State Medical Journal*, November 1977, pp. 12-14.

Valle, S.K. Types of confrontation and level of counselor functioning. Unpublished research, Mount Pleasant Hospital, Lynn, Mass., 1978.

Valle, S.K. & Anthony, W. The effects of alcohol training methods on helping skills-functioning of alcoholism counselors. *Maryland State Medical Journal*, May 1977, pp. 31-33.

Valle, S.K. & Marinelli, R. Training in human relations skills as a preferred mode of treatment for married couples. *Journal of Marriage and Family Counseling*, October 1975, pp. 359-365.

VanHoose, W. & Kottler, J. *Ethical and Legal Issues in Counseling and Psychotherapy*. San Francisco: Jossey-Bass, 1977.

Vinter, R.D. The social structure of service. In A.J. Kahn (Ed.): *Issues in American Social Work*. New York: Columbia Univ. Press, 1959.

Weldon v. Virginia State Board of Psychologist Examiners, Corporation Court, Newport News, Va., Oct. 4, 1974.

Yalom, Irvin. *The Theory and Practice of Group Psychotherapy*. New York: Basic Books, 1970.

Zaro, J., Barach, R., Nedelman, D., & Dreiblatt, I. *A Guide for Beginning Psychotherapists*. London: Cambridge Univ. Press, 1977.

NAME INDEX

A

Abrams, G. M., 112, 123, 151
Ajzen, R., 77, 151
Altucher, N., 112, 151
Anthony, W. A., xi, 12, 34, 36, 38, 39, 151, 156
Arbuckle, D. S., 18, 112, 151
Archer, J., 121, 151

B

Barach, R., 156
Barclay, J. R., 94, 151
Bellucci, J. E., 120, 151
Benjamin, A., 77, 151
Berenson, B. G., 151, 152
Berenson, D. H., 31, 38, 39, 42, 44, 114, 127, 128, 129, 130, 132, 151
Biddle, B. J., 154
Blocher, D. H., 95, 151
Bower, G., 127, 151
Bower, S., 127, 151
Boyd, J. D., 111, 112, 113, 120, 121, 152
Bramer, L., 146, 152
Brown, W. T., 30, 31, 152
Buchheimer, A., 123, 153
Burthe, L., 154

C

Carkhuff, Robert R., xi, 30, 31, 32, 33, 38, 39, 42, 44, 49, 114, 127, 128, 129, 130, 132, 151, 152
Clinebell, H., 126, 152

D

Daubner, E. S., 78, 152
Daubner, E. V., 78, 152
Delaney, D. J., 124, 144, 153

Dell Orto, Art, xi, 39, 151
Delworth, 30, 152
Dendy, R. F., 121, 152
Dreiblatt, I., 147, 156
Dyer, W., 127, 153

E

Eisenberg, S., 124, 144, 153
Ellis, A., 90, 153
Esser, B. F., 155

F

Farrand, Gail, xii
Forster, J., 16, 153
Franks, V., 154
Freileigh, P. W., 123, 153

G

Gartner, A., 30, 31, 153
Geller, M. H., 143, 154
Gerrein, J. R., 12, 155
Goldstein, A. P., 93, 153
Gross, R., 153
Gross, S., 17, 18, 153
Guy, E., 127, 153

H

Harmin, M., 88, 89, 155
Hefele, T. J., 39, 153
Hoffman, A. M., 36, 153
Howard, D., 126, 153
Howard, N., 126, 153
Howe, C. W., 88, 155
Hughes, E., 153
Hughes, Harold E., viii, xi, 10
Hultman, K., 90, 153

157

I

Ivey, A. E., 120, 153

J

Johnson, D. E., 140, 153
Johnson, V. E., 94, 95, 99, 103, 126, 153

K

Kadushin, A., 111, 153
Kagan, N., 121, 122, 151, 153, 154
Kahn, A. J., 156
Kaslow, F., 124, 151, 154
Kell, B. L., 112, 140, 154, 155
Kemp, C. G., 89, 154
Kennedy, E., 136, 137, 154
Kent, L., 8, 30, 47, 155
Kirschenbaum, H., 88, 155
Korchin, S. J., 142, 154
Kottler, J., 76, 77, 78, 80, 156
Krathwohl, D. R., 121, 122, 153, 154
Kruger, D. H., 155
Kutzik, A., 110, 154

L

Lasky, Robert, xi, 39, 143, 151, 154
Lazarus, A., 33, 93, 154
Liftik, J., 12, 155
Lister, J., 31, 49, 156
Lopes, Manny, xii

M

Mann, C. H., 124, 154
Mann, J. H., 124, 154
Manohar, V., 12, 155
Marcus, G., 111, 154
Marinelli, Robert, xi, 39, 151, 156
Maslach, C., 63, 154
McGowan, J. F., 78, 154
Mendelsohn, G. A., 143, 154
Miller, R., 122, 154
Mitchell, K., 127, 128, 129, 130, 132, 151
Moore, W., 10, 154
Muchowski, Patrice, xii, 127, 154
Mueller, W. J., 112, 140, 154, 155

N

Nedelman, D., 147, 156

O

Older, H., 126, 155
Osterman, P., 153

P

Patterson, C. H., 153, 155
Phillips, D., 126, 155
Pierce, R., 33, 152
Pietrofessa, J. J., 80, 155
Powell, D., 116, 155
Power, P., 39, 151

R

Raths, L. E., 88, 89, 155
Riessman, R., 30, 31, 153
Roemer, R., 18, 155
Rogers, Carl R., 18, 32, 107, 155
Rokeach, M., 88, 155
Rosenberg, C. M., 12, 155

S

Sapolsky, A., 143, 155
Schauble, F. C., 121, 122, 154
Scheibe, K. E., 88, 155
Schmidt, L. D., 78, 154
Shear, Maurice, xi
Shimberg, B., 18, 155
Shostrum, C., 146, 152
Simon, S. B., 88, 89, 155
Solomone, P., 10, 155
Spaniol, L., 151
Spivack, J. D., 121, 155
Staub, G., 8, 30, 47, 155.
Stefflre, B., 95, 156
Sue, D., 46, 156
Sweeney, T., 21, 156

T

Thomas, E. J., 154
Thurber, Art, xi

Thursz, D., 48, 156
Truax, C. B., 31, 49, 114, 152, 156

V

Valle, Mary, xii
Valle, Stephen K., vii, 8, 12, 31, 34, 35, 36, 38, 39, 45, 48, 127, 128, 154, 156
VanHoose, W., 76, 77, 78, 80, 156
Vestermark, M. J., 94, 95, 99, 103, 140, 153
Vinter, R. D., 111, 156
Vriend, J., 80, 155

W

Witmer, J., 21, 156

Y

Yalom, Irvin, 140, 156

Z

Zaro, J., 147, 156

SUBJECT INDEX

A

Accreditation
defined, 16, 17, 23
of training programs, 23-25
standards developed by EAAETP, 24-25
Al-Anon, impact consumers in, 47
Alcoholics Anonymous
counseling versus 12-step work, 98-99
impact consumers in, 47
Alcoholism counseling
as a profession, 9-13 (see also Profession of alcoholism counseling)
Carkhuff Model (see Carkhuff Model)
central goal of, 97
counselor encapsulation as barrier to, 96-97
counselor overinvolvement, 97-98
defined, 100
development of profession, vii
divided loyalties, 98-99
involvement consumer in, 47-48
mission of, 149
Model for, 38-45
obstacles to effective, 92-108 (see also Obstacles)
for client, 99-108
for counselor, 92-99
phases of learning, 39
supervision in, 114-116 (see also Supervision)
12-step AA work versus, 98-99
Alcoholism counselors
accreditation of, 23-25
alcoholism helpers (see Alcoholism helpers)
background of, vii
burn-out, 61-74 (see also Burn-out)
certification of, 16
clients' rights, 47-48
commitment and dedication to, 11

consumerism and, 46-48
credentialing, 14-28 (see also Credentialing)
defining function of, 15
development personal theory of, 94-95
identity problems, 17
identifying potential, 29, 37 (see also Alcoholism helpers)
importance of, 8
interpersonal skills researched, 39
obstacles facing, 92-99 (see also Obstacles)
professional counselor legislation and, 20-21
role confusion, 92-94
role of, 7, 8
role of relationship to setting, 92-93
Alcoholism helpers
Carkhuff Model (see Carkhuff Model)
conclusion study of, 37
effective functioning levels after training, 36-37
effective helping and skills level, 39
effects subjectivity and emotionalism in, 30
facilitative conditions necessary in, 32-33
facilitative dimensions, 32-34
functioning effectiveness study, 34
identification effective helping, 32-33
identification potential, 29-37
ingredients in effective helping relationships, 33-34
paraprofessional movement, 30-32 (see also Paraprofessionals)
problems negativism, 30
recovered alcoholics as, 29-30
recovering versus degreed, 34-36
results research study, 35-36
training of, 36-38
American Association of Marriage and Family Counselors, credentialing, 21

161

American Association of Sex Educators
and Counselors, certification, 21
American Personnel and Guidance Association
Commission on Licensure, 19-20
professional counselor licensure position, 19-20

B

Behavioral approach to supervision, 113
basis, 113
focus, 113
steps in process, 113
Burn-out in counselors, 61, 74
causes, 64-68
disillusionment, 65-66
factors contributing, 65-68
lack client appreciation, 66
lack status and prestige, 67-68
limitations, 68
personal problems, 65
self inadequacy, 66-67
defined, 62-63
description process, 63
effect on clients, 63-64
effect on colleagues, 64
frequency occurance, 61
prevention, 62-73, 74
evaluation position, 73-74
identification goals, 73-74
knowledgeable about position, 73
maintaining personal growth, 74
treatment, 68-72
accepting limitations, 69
asking for help, 69
continuation work, 70
diversification responsibilities, 71-72
recognizable symptoms, 68-69
time-outs, 70-71
use of, 72-73
vulnerability counselors to, 62

C

Carkhuff Supervisory Training Model
basis, 40, 114
confrontation, 130-133
emphasis, 44-45, 114

helpee dimensions, 39-41
action phase, 40-41, 114, 130-131
exploration, 40, 130
measurement, 41
phases, 39-40
responses, 130
self-understanding, 130
understanding, 40, 131
helper dimensions, 40, 41-44, 114, 129-130
accountability, 41
attending skills, 43
communication respect, 42
concreteness, 42
confrontation, 130-131
empathy, 42, 114
genuineness, 42, 114
helping skills, 42-43, 114, 130
initiating skills, 44, 114, 130
measurement, 41
operationalizing goals, 44
personalizing skills, 43
premature confrontations, 130
relationship skills to learning, 44
responding skills, 43-44, 114, 130
skills needed, 41, 44, 114
helping defined, 40
implication, 132, 133
sequence types confrontation, 131-132
presentation illustration, 132
use, 38-39, 45
Certification
advantages of, 26
defined, 16, 23
perspectives, 26
Confidentiality, 83-86
as a counseling process, 84
concern of clients, 83-84
counselor knowledge regulation regarding, 86
criminal act threat and, 84-85
defined, 84
H.E.W. regulations, 84
referral data and, 85
research data and, 85
written consent forms and release of, 85-86
Confrontation counseling, 126-133
as unnecessary, 127-128

basis, 130
didactic, 129, 131
encouragement to action type, 129
experiential, 128-129, 131
functions of, 128
implications, 132-133
sequence use of various types, 129-130,
  130-131 (*see also* Carkhuff Model)
specific therapeutic approaches and, 127
strength type, 129, 131
types of, 128-129
 didactic, 129
 encouragement to action, 129
 experiential, 128-129
 sequence of effectiveness, 129-130
 strength, 129
 weakness, 129
use of, 126-127, 128, 130
weakness type, 129, 131
Consumerism in counseling, 46-56
and alcoholism services, 46-48
concerns about consumerism, 54-56
consumer questions, 46
defined, 46-47
goal of, 47
guidelines for consumers, 53-54
Taunton model program, 48-52 (*see also*
  Taunton model)
use printed handout by counselors, 53
Co-therapy method of supervision, 122-
123
advantages, 122
difficulties, 123
Counseling, professional (*see* Professional
  counseling)
Credentialing, 14-28
accreditation, 16, 23 (*see also* Accreditation)
accreditation of training programs, 23-25
as extension training, 27-28
as recognition, 15
basic needs fulfilled by, 22-23
certification, 16, 26
competency and, 17-18, 23
dangers of, 18
definition, 15
Department H.E.W., proposal for, 21-
22
forms of, 16, 19

function credentialing board, 27
identity alcoholism counselors and, 17
importance of, 14-15
issues, 25-28
licensure, 16, 18
means of, 16
models for, 21-22
need for, 11, 12, 14-15
National Institute on Alcohol Abuse and
  Alcoholism study, 22-23
of professional counselors, 19
perspectives, 14-19
problems defining function, 15-16
recent developments, 19-23
registration, 16
third party reimbursement and, 15, 21
to protect consumer, 14-15, 23
use credentialing commission, 27
value of, 14-15

E

Eastern Area Alcohol Education and
  Training Program
accreditation council function, 24, 25
accreditation standards developed by,
  24-25
basis of, 24-25
importance, 24
primary purpose, 24
specific standards, 24-25
survey and review process, 25
preceptorship program, 117-119
agreement used, 119
content, 118
need for, 116-117
purposes, 117
requirements for preceptor, 118-119
role preceptor, 118
Ethics in counseling, 75-91
areas requiring specific standards of, 87
basis, 78
defined, 77-78
development casebook standards of, 88
establishment committee on, 87-88
establishment comprehensive code of,
  86-87
limitations, 78
need to consider, 75-76

neutrality of counselors, 76-77
perspective on unethical behavior, 79-88
  (*see also* Unethical behavior)
perspectives on standards of, 77-79
problems in development, 79
professional dangers protected by, 78-79
purpose professional ethical code, 78
used, 78
values in counseling, 88-91 (*see also*
  Values in counseling)

F

Functional professional, use of term, 31

H

Hughes Act of 1970, 32

I

Incompetence, defined, 80
Incompetent behavior counselors, 79-80
Integrative approach to supervision, 113-
  114
  Carkhuff Training Model, 114
International Transactional Analysis Association, certification, 21
Interpersonal process recall method of supervision, 121-122
description, 121, 122
principal objectives, 122
questions used, 121-122

L

Licensure
defined, 16, 18, 23
of professional counselors, 19-20

M

Microtraining, 120-121
definition, 120
steps used, 120-121
use, 121

N

National Association of Social Work,

concept of supervision, 111
National Commission for Credentialing
  Alcoholism Counselors, function of
  proposed, 23
National Institute on Alcohol Abuse and
  Alcoholism, Credentialing alcoholism
  counselors study, 22-23

O

Obstacles to effective counseling, 92-108
client ambivalence toward change, 102-
  106
  acceptance need to change, 104
  action steps for change, 105
  counselor technique used to resolve,
    104-105
  denial as defense, 103
  facilitating decision to change, 104
  recognition of need to change, 103
  stages in resolution of, 103
for the client, 99-108
  ambivalence toward change, 102-106
  client expectations, 99-100
  client manipulations, 106-107
  defensive behaviors, 106-107
  losses with change, 103
  negative experiences, 100-101
  placing counselor on defensive, 106
  positive experience, 101
  previous experience, 101
for the counselor, 92-99
  counselor encapsulation, 96-97
  counselor overinvolvement, 97-98
  development working theory of coun-
    seling, 95
  divided loyalties, 98-99
  generalist versus specialist, 93-94
  indeterminate philosophical base, 94-96
  need personal theory of counseling, 94-
    95
  role confusion, 92-94

P

Paraprofessionals
defined, 30-31
effectiveness of, 31
functioning level after training, 36

impact of, 31-32
use in helping alcoholics, 32
Peer group supervision, 123-124
  defined, 123
  factors determining effectiveness, 123-124
  uses, 123, 124
Profession of alcoholism counseling
  advocates against, 7
  assessment of characteristics, 11-12
  characteristics of, 9-13
  code of ethics, 11, 12
  commitment and dedication, 11
  credentialing system need, 11, 12 (*see also* Credentialing)
  definition role and, 13
  federal funding and, 12
  future tasks for, 11-12
  identifying characteristics, 11
  knowledge and skills, 11-12
  national organization need, 11, 13
  professional journal need, 13
  rationale for, 8-9
  secondary motivations, 9-10
  thought against, 7
  training and, 11, 12
  traits characteristic of, 11
Professional counseling
  ethical codes for, 77-79
  regulation of, 19, 20
  third-party reimbursement and, 21
  trends legislation practice of, 20
Professions
  characteristics, 10-12
  motivations for development of, 9-10
  nature of, 10
  primary motivation for, 9
  regulation of, 19
  results of, 9-10
Psychotherapeutic approach to supervision, 112-113
  adaptations, 112
    classic approach, 112
    metatherapy concept, 112
  focus, 112-113
  goal, 112

R

Registration, 16, 23

Rehabilitation, involvement consumer in, 47-48
Rehabilitation counselor, certification of, 21
Reluctant clients, 133-140
  comparison to resistant client, 135-136
  counseling and, 139
  counselor's reaction to, 134-135
  definition, 133
  effect type referral on, 134, 135
  expressions client and counselor, 134-135
Resistant clients, 133-140
  as defensive behavior, 135
  carefree defense used by, 138
  comparison reluctant client, 135-136
  counseling and, 139-140
  definition, 133-134
  expression, 136-137
  generalizations and vagueness used by, 138
  intellectualizing by, 137
  monopolizing talkativeness by, 137
  reaction counselor to, 135-136
  reasons for, 134, 135, 136
  responses used by, 138-139
  seductive behavior, 139
  silence use by, 136-137
Role of alcoholism counselor, 7, 8-9
  need define, 13

S

Supervision, 109-125
  clinical preceptorship, 116-119
  definition, 109-110, 114-115
  Eastern Area Alcohol Education and Training Program, Inc., 116-119
  in alcoholism counseling, 114-116
    components of, 115-116
    functions, 116
    relationship meaning and setting, 114-115
  medical model of, 110
  methods of, 119-125
    case-conference, 119, 120
    co-therapy, 122-123
    interpersonal process recall, 121-122
    microtraining, 120-121
    one-to-one interaction, 119-120

peer-group supervision, 123-124
role playing, 124
need for, 109
psychological model, 111-114
 approaches, 111
 behaviorial approach, 113
 Carkhuff Training Model, 114
 counselor supervision, 111, 112
 integrative approach, 113-114
 psychotherapeutic approach, 112
social work concept of, 110-111

T

Taunton Center
 advisory board, 51-52
 advocacy function of consumers, 49
 description, 48-49
 principles of consumer motivation, 50
 Taunton Model developed (*see* Taunton
  Model)
 therapy forms available, 49
Taunton Model program, 48-52, 54-55
 consumer failure, 55
 overzealous helper, 54-55
 problem areas, 54-55
 professional resistance, 55
 role consumers, 49-50
  advisory board membership, 51-52
  as technician, 51
  community staff member, 51
  recipient direct services, 51
  therapeutic aide, 52
Taunton Center (*see* Taunton Center)
Team members roles, 8
Termination, 140-148
 as a commencement, .140
 as accomplishment, 147
 feelings of client, 141
 guidelines for, 147-148
 hesitation of client, 141
 importance effective, 147
 importance good procedures, 140
 initiation of, 147-148
 of unsuccessful counseling, 141-142
 premature, 144-145
  by client, 145
  external events, 144
  reaction of client, 144

 reaction of counselor, 144-145
 reasons for, 140-143
  client dislike of counselor, 142-143
  goals achieved, 140-141
 · manipulative act of client, 142
  unsuccessful counseling, 142
 resistance to, 143-144
  by clients, 143
  by counselor, 143
  recurrence symptoms, 143-144
 sense of loss upon, 141
 specific guidelines for, 148
 techniques for, 146-147
  by summarization, 146
  by time limits, 146
  of a case, 146-147
  of a session, 146
Training programs
 accreditation of, 23-25
 credentialing of, 25
 EAAETP accreditation standards developed, 24-25
 primary purpose, 24
 role of, 23
 specific standards, 24-25
 survey and review process, 25
 use term accredition, 23
Treatment issues, 126-148
 confrontation, 126-133 (*see also*
  Confrontation)
 counseling reluctant clients, 133-140 (*see
  also* Reluctant clients)
 counseling resistant clients, 133-140 (*see
  also* Resistant clients)
 termination in counseling, 140-148

U

Unethical behavior, 79-88
 confidentiality issues, 83-86, (*see also*
  Confidentiality)
 encouraging dependency in clients, 82
 incompetent behavior versus, 79-80
 mistakes versus, 80
 operating beyond one's competency, 83
 overidentification with clients, 81-82
 overinvolvement with clients, 81
Unethical counselor, defined, 80
U.S. Department of Health, Education

and Welfare
credentialing proposed by, 21-22
regulation confidentiality of records, 84

V

Values in counseling, 88-91 (*see also* Ethics in counseling)
client evaluation values, 89-90

conflict as young counselors, 91
counselor awareness personal values, 89, 91
relationship values and behavior, 88-89, 91
use as a defense, 90-91
use as behavior motivator, 90
use to preserve self image, 90-91